TABLE OF CONTENTS

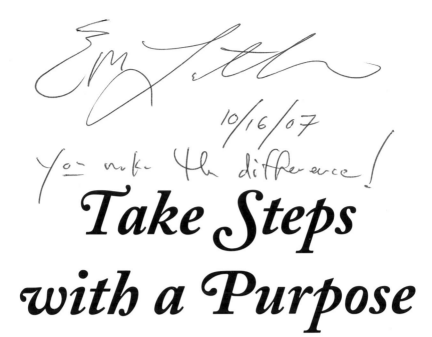

Take Steps
with a Purpose

A book by
Eric M. Latham

Based on his Walk Across America
for Cancer Research

www.walkaboutamerica.com

ISBN: 1-4243-0760-0

Photographs were taken by the author. Matt Brennan contributed photographs for the "Bridge for a Cure" section.

Cover design by the author and Fine Line Design, Winnipeg, Manitoba. Text design by Fine Line Design.

Printed in Canada

Dedicated to the thousands of people
I met along the way,
and the thousands I've yet to meet.

PROLOGUE

Life is full of tragedy and triumph. It's our ability to realize the exceptional moments that makes life worth living. Somehow I convinced myself that walking from the Atlantic Ocean to the Pacific would be a dream I was capable of accomplishing, but without passion, a dream is just a thought. That's how it all started, just a thought. What if I could walk across our great nation for a cause?

I've always wanted to fight for a cause. After graduating high school, my dad told me I could get a job or go to college, get a job or fend off reality for a few more years. The choice was easy. I was curious, and I wasn't quite ready for a blatantly systematic lifestyle. Plus, I liked the idea of meeting similar beings who were interested in challenging government, institutions, and everything we claim to be factual.

Four years later, I was sitting in an auditorium at graduation, among hundreds of "twenty-somethings" not like me. I could have been alone. The commencement speaker rapped about the key to success and the future. Truly, for the first time in my life, I was disappointed. Sure, I'd taken part in student government, rallied other students, and even traveled many miles to protest the cruel treatment of animals at a pet store chain, but I hadn't really challenged a damn thing as an undergrad at Virginia Tech. The man at the podium must have made a clever remark because the crowd erupted in laughter. I glared at him like a spoiled child. It wasn't ok.

Well, we graduated anyway, and I got my piece of paper. It put me thousands of dollars in debt, but school loans weren't about to keep me from seeing the world. Shortly after graduation, I was on a plane to France to improve my conversational ability to speak the language. It would be nice to pick up the people's parler, not the formal tongue we're taught in U.S. public schools. (Excluding, of course, what we call French-style kissing, which seems "au natural" to most Americans).

I was lying to myself. It wasn't about learning a second language to improve my resume. I wanted more. I wanted worldly perspective. So, I arrived in Paris with a little over two hundred dollars. At the time, the Euro was whipping the greenback. Whether I liked it or not, I'd have to get a job. I could either return to the United States after an expensive, extended weekend in Paris, or I could "franco-fi" and join the French workforce.

The woman I was staying with in the romantic city suggested that I head to the southern part of the country to pick strawberries. Immediately my ego took over. What? Pick strawberries? Are you kidding me? I had a degree, but I wasn't ready to go home.

I took the TGV (Train Grande Vitesse) to the city of Avignon. For two days I was homeless, wandering the city by day and spending my nights at Palais de Paupes, mingling with so many others who called the medieval monument home. The French were alive. Every day, someone or some group was up in arms over civil rights or an election. I was envious. These people were marching and chanting phrases I couldn't understand. But that didn't matter. I saw passion burning in their eyes, literally during one protest. They'd lit a coffin on fire and placed it on the steps of City Hall. Sounds serious, but it was peaceful. Eventually, the crowd dispersed, leaving only echoes bouncing off the ramparts and ashes from the coffin dancing in the breeze. Everything was ok. Nothing had changed, except for me. I felt invigorated.

Without a work permit, I stubbornly clawed my way into a job as a bartender at the Red Lion Inn and for the next four months lived with Kamalji Sen, a 60-year-old man from India. During that time, I learned that foreign views of the United States weren't always favorable. After spitting on me, one man contended that Americans were weak, hedonistic people. It was disturbing; not the saliva dripping from my hair, but whether many people outside the U.S. really felt that way.

Upon my return to the States, I found myself mentally removed from American culture, metaphorically homeless, examining the way we live. I wanted to move to a unique city that would expose me to a side of our society I'd never seen before.

One of my sisters, Brookelyn, lived in Las Vegas, Nevada. It was on the other side of the country, but I thought I'd give it a try. Living in the Sin City was unique, all right—a city with a split personality. You have the glitz and glamour of the casino-resort industry and what remains, carbonized.

After a few odd jobs, I decided to put my communications studies degree to use. The investigative department at KTNV-TV, the local ABC news affiliate, was doing a story on my sister. Some water softener company was apparently running a vacation scam, and Brookelyn called them on it. Those poor souls, if they only knew who they were dealing with.

When the producer came to interview my sister, I interjected my love for writing. A couple of months later, KTNV hired me as an associate news producer for their investigative department. It was very exciting at first. We were reporting the truth and helping people. Then the mid-day news producer position opened up. The assistant news director asked if I'd take it. What an opportunity! Here I was, 22 years old, with my own show in a top-50 market. Little did I know, I was in for a bumpy ride; maybe responsibility I wasn't ready for.

Months went by, and I began to wonder how I was making an impact on my community or on my country. I started looking for something new. I'd heard about people teaching English in other countries, so I decided to do some research. After speaking with several companies, I chose one out of New York City. The plan was to teach English at a University in the northeast part of China, between Mongolia and Russia. The contract was straightforward. I would pay for the flight to Beijing, and they would reimburse me when I got there. It also said that they would obtain all documents needed to enter and work in the country. I signed the contract and faxed it to Li Ma, the director of the program. She sent me an email saying that she had received it. In three months, I quit my job, left my apartment, and cancelled my cell phone. A few days before my 23rd birthday, I said goodbye to my girlfriend as I boarded a plane that would take me halfway around the world. I felt great. What an experience this was going to be. A new language, a new culture, a new world.

On the flight over, the flight attendants served us Cup-O-Noodles for a snack. For lunch, they served Cup-O-Noodles. For Dinner, they served Cup-O-Noodles and a fortune cookie. As luck would have it, the catering company that served the airline was on strike.

Twelve hours later, the plane landed in Beijing. It was the longest and most uncomfortable flight I'd ever been on, but I didn't care. I'd taken a chance, and this experience would change my life forever. I was taking on the world.

Something didn't sit right with the woman at the customs counter when I handed her my passport. Without looking me in the eyes, she picked up the telephone and made a quick call. A man in uniform with a large gun hanging from a strap around his shoulders approached and motioned for me to follow him. He led me to an elevated kiosk busy with what looked like military personnel. A man behind the desk spoke to me in Chinese. It was obvious that I hadn't learned a thing from the "Learn Mandarin the Easy Way" tapes I had checked out from a public library in Las Vegas.

Finally, I took out a phone number that Li Ma instructed me to call when I arrived at the airport. The man at the desk punched in the digits, spoke a few words into the receiver, and handed me the phone.

"Hello?"

"Eric, where are you?" It was Li Ma.

"For some reason they won't let me through customs," I said, hoping for an explanation.

"Let me talk to them," she said.

I held up the phone. The military man plucked it out of my hand and listened for half a minute. Suddenly, he was screaming into the receiver. He handed it back to me with a stern poker face. It didn't look good. I watched for any 'tells' and listened.

"Hello, Li?"

"Eric," she replied, "There's been a horrible mistake."

"What?" I said.

"You won't be allowed in the country."

"What—Why not?"

"You don't have the right paperwork," she said.

"But—"

She interrupted me, "I'm sorry, there's been a horrible mistake." Then she hung up.

There was a sinking feeling in my stomach as I handed the phone back to the military man. He made another call, and within minutes I was being escorted by three other men with guns that dangled around their necks like holiday ornaments. At six feet four inches, I was quite a bit taller than each of them. They took me through several hallways to a small cement room, which wasn't very well furnished. There were a few plastic chairs and a wooden desk that looked like it had been through a tornado. One of the men stayed with me while the other two stepped outside the door. The babysitter motioned me to sit in a chair.

Half an hour went by before anything happened. A man, not in military garb, entered and pulled up a chair next to me. He introduced himself as an employee of the airline. He spoke English well. With a "let's get down to business" look, the man pulled up a chair in front of me and started asking questions about my purpose in China and my relationship with the United States government. For my first time in the country, it wasn't the warmest welcome. When he seemed to be through, I had a question for him.

"Why are you doing this?"

"Because you're American," he replied simply, as if I should've already known the answer. I was shocked and speechless. A pregnant silence ensued for a full five seconds before he continued. "You'll get on the same plane and fly back to the United States."

Initially I was confused. Was this really happening? The three military men had gathered around me once again.

"They will escort you through security," added the interrogator, as he exited the room, which seemed a lot smaller now that my blood was boiling.

They led me through the metal detectors and made sure I got on the plane. It made me nervous, but I don't know why. There were no secrets. I gave up my life in Las Vegas to teach English in China. I signed a contract.

I've never been so miserable at 40,000 feet above the earth. I'd just been kicked out of China, and I didn't really know why. I was angry, and it didn't help that I was surrounded by hundreds of Chinese, headed for the U.S. Hopefully they weren't treated the way I was in their country.

I tried contacting Li Ma when I got back, but she never responded. I felt lost. Las Vegas would never be the same, so I decided to leave. With China and the Sin City in my rear view, I drove across the country in less than three days. After arriving at my Mom's house in Tennessee, I kept thinking about my cross-country road trip, wishing I'd taken more time to meet new people along the way.

Out of money, I moved to Asheville, North Carolina. The city had a lot to offer a young person. I even found some work in radio reporting and a room to rent. I became friends with Andy, the owner of the house where I was staying.

One day, I came home after spending all day working on a story about second amendment rights. Andy was heating up some soup in the kitchen. He was always interested in the latest topic I was reporting on. We talked about the right to bear arms and what we wanted out of life. I told him about college. I told him about France, Las Vegas, and China. I told him about driving across the country and wanting more. Before taking another bite of soup, he said, "Why not walk?"

"Walk across the country?" I asked chuckling.

"Why not?"

"That's a pretty long walk," I said, as if he didn't know.

Andy thought about it for a second and nodded with a big smile. I couldn't help but shake my head and laugh. At first, the idea of walking across the country sounded ridiculous, but as the day went on, it actually started making sense. I thought, "What if I did it to raise money for a cause?"

Lying in bed that night, I wondered what I'd call my walk. It would be about people. It would be about the importance of service to community and country. It would be about America. That's when it hit me. I'd call it **Walk About America.**

My time in Asheville was short-lived. Within a few weeks, I moved to Richmond, Virginia where I created and developed Walk About America, an organization dedicated to invigorating the generous nature of Americans by enhancing community awareness and involvement. My mom being a skin cancer survivor, I dedicated the 2005 campaign to joining the fight against cancer. I also spent time volunteering at Massey Cancer Center in Richmond. While I was volunteering, I became friends with many people who were suffering, but no patient had an impact on me like Austin Staples.

Austin was a 12-year-old boy from the Richmond area being treated for inoperable brain tumors. After hearing about my idea to walk across the country for cancer research, some of his family asked if I'd visit Austin and his mother in the hospital. I went three times and only once was he actually conscious. Even then, his recent surgery and high doses of medication were too much.

As I tried to tell Austin about the walk, he mumbled and moaned in agony. I turned to his mother, who managed to smile despite the tears welling up in her eyes. There was so much pain in the room. It wasn't fair. I felt like Austin had been cheated in life. What had he done to deserve all that? Looking into Austin's eyes, I understood how he could endure so much pain. I'd never seen such amazing strength and courage in my life. At that moment, I knew I was walking across the country for Austin.

The next weekend, I was participating in a walk to raise money for Austin's treatment. Hundreds of people showed up, some who knew him, many who didn't. The community had really come together to support my new friend. We were all going to help him beat cancer.

Just as the race was about to begin, the organizer of the event stood up in front of the crowd and said something I'll never forget.

"For those of you who don't know, Austin died yesterday."

My heart crumbled like an aluminum can. I couldn't believe it. I'd just seen Austin that week. We were going to save him.

The gunshot that started the race rattled me back to reality. I really didn't feel like walking anymore. It didn't seem right. Just then, an elderly lady walked by and smiled at me.

"You gotta start moving your feet before you can get anywhere," she said.

❧

CHAPTER 1

The Tar Heel State

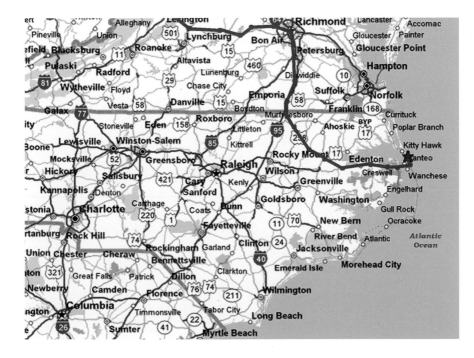

The bulbous steel hook whipped past my head like the iron fist of a champion boxer. All my senses were razor sharp and racing. I could see myself lying bludgeoned on the side of the road. I could taste the blood in my mouth from the direct hit. I could smell the diesel fumes and hear the rumble of the big rig engine trailing off in the distance. I could feel my heart pounding on my chest cavity like a madman. Having such an imagination is dangerous; so is walking on the side of the road.

It had been a long day. I'd completed 22 miles of a 27-mile walk to Windsor, North Carolina. There was about a foot of pavement between the fading white line and an uneven ditch covered in foliage. I liked to walk against the traffic for a couple of reasons. I wanted people to see my shirt, and I thought it would be safer knowing what was coming my way.

Logging trucks had been passing me all day. They'd blow by at 50 or 60 miles an hour. Most of them would cross the yellow line to make sure they wouldn't hit me, but not this one. Maybe he didn't see me. Maybe there was more money to be made if he arrived at his destination any quicker. Maybe he just didn't care. One thing's for sure: If that hook on an eight-foot belt, dangling off the end of his truck had found my face, it would have killed me.

~

The moment I cracked the window, a blast of wet wind rushed over my face and through my hair. I could smell the sea salt and hear the surf pounding the beach. As we paralleled the Atlantic, searching for a hotel, I asked Ma to pull the car over. Quickly, I removed my shoes and socks and made a dash for the water. It had been a while since I'd seen the ocean.

"Hello, old friend," I whispered, staring out across the velvet blue ripples, sifting my toes through sand. This was where an average grain was going to get his start.

By the time Ma and I had reached the Outer Banks, it was dark and rainy. We got there a day and half early so we could spend some time together.

The extra day also gave me time to make final preparations. On commencement eve, Ma and I were busy ironing black letters on two yellow t-shirts. It was the kind of tedious work that could drive a person crazy. With a proud, motherly approval, Ma held up the first shirt. It spelled out:

CANCER RESEACH WALKER

Maybe it was just the iron, but there appeared to be steam rising off of my mother when she noticed the error. We deflated in disappointment. We made sure to include *all* of the letters on the second shirt.

The hotel room phone rang at 6 am. Our wake-up call was right on time. I jumped out of bed with Christmas morning excitement and flung the door open to find a glorious surprise. Ever since we arrived in the Outer Banks, it had rained, but on this morning, my morning, the sun had paved a golden highway over the water, right to our doorstep.

Sunrise in Nags Head, North Carolina on April 14, 2005.

For months I'd dreamed about that day and how things would go. Everybody from Massey Cancer Center would be there—cancer survivors, their families, caregivers, and volunteers. I even contacted some local media, but nobody could make it. Nobody showed up for the big day. It was just Ma and I.

I handed her the camera and positioned myself at the edge of the water despite the biting cold temperature.

"Wave," she said cheerfully.

I obeyed my mother until she lowered the camera.

"Did you get it?" I shouted over a strong bluster. It was evident by the confused look on her face that she wasn't exactly sure.

She yelled back, "Let's take one more."

I waved again and waited. She held the camera up to her face for at least 20 seconds. For some reason it wasn't working. I put down my side bag and walked over to her. Ma handed me the camera, shaking her head in disbelief. There was no major malfunction. The batteries were dead, so I popped in a fresh set.

I turned around just in time to see a huge wave smash into my side bag, about twenty yards away. What's worse is that it was being carried out to sea. My eyes bulged, and I nearly choked on several expletives. I dropped my pack and darted towards the water in my best Baywatch impression. With little hesitation, I high-stepped through the waves and snagged my side bag, swearing the whole way. Maybe it was better the media didn't show up.

The ocean hissed and fizzled over the cruel joke. I sloshed back over to Ma, who was trying to hide the humor behind her hand. My boots were soaked, the bag was waterlogged, and several items inside it were ruined. It was a heck of a way to start. Still, we got the photo, and Walk About America 2005 was officially underway.

Ma waved as I walked away. She admitted later that she was crying, not because one of her children was walking off into the great unknown, but because she was worried about my left knee. Just three months earlier, I'd had surgery on it to remove a chunk of bone about the size of a quarter. Worrying that it might cause permanent damage, my doctor asked me not to walk. I asked him for the bone chunk and carried it with me whole way.

The first 60 minutes of the walk may have been the most challenging part of the entire journey. It was no stroll around the block. Suddenly this great undertaking was real, and it hit me as I crossed the Causeway, a bridge I thought had a rather fitting name.

Walking off the beach in Nags Head, North Carolina on April 14, 2005.

Skepticism began swimming around in my head, evoking a major question:

"What the hell was I doing out there?"

There I was, 23 years old with a college degree, and it was my job to walk. I was a professional pedestrian. I guess it was more complex than that, with the creation of Walk About America, but I definitely wasn't making a living. Nobody was paying me to walk. It was pro-bono work in the fullest sense, but what bothered me most was that I didn't believe in myself. I didn't think I could walk across the United States, with or without a cause.

It was about noon when I reached Manns Harbor, my first scheduled stop. There wasn't much: a church, a couple of trailers, and one convenience store. A bell jingled when I opened the door, announcing my arrival. A man behind the cash register looked up. I guessed he was in his early 30's, uncombed blond hair thinning at the front, short and stout, but not like a teapot. There was no handle. I smiled. He didn't. I tried to be friendly and make conversation.

"So this is Manns Harbor?"

He nodded without looking up. I made my way to the cooler for a sports drink, nearly knocking over several snack display stands with my awkward pack. That got his attention. He glanced at my shirt as I approached the counter.

"Cancer research walker, huh?" He had a thick southern accent.

"Yep," I was anxious to explain myself. "I'm walking from ocean to ocean to raise money for cancer research."

"Oh." He didn't believe me. "Where'd ya start?"

"Nags Head today," I said enthusiastically, handing him the money for the beverage.

"Got a long way to go," he said in a rather mocking tone. I just smiled and looked him straight in the eye without responding.

"You're crazy," he said with a fading smile, "But I appreciate what you're doing."

In a few seconds, he continued, "Come outside with me for a minute."

I lugged my pack outside and took a seat on an old wooden barrel. It was nice to sit down. My feet were already sore. The cashier soon followed holding a cigarette. He fumbled through his pockets, thrilled when he found a lighter. He lit up, took a drag, and let out a huge sigh of relief along with a plume of second-hand smoke.

Paul in Manns Harbor, North Carolina.

After taking a long, deep breath he said, "Probably shouldn't be smoking with you walking for cancer and all—especially since my mom died of lung cancer."

He told me what he remembered about his mom, about her experience with cancer, and how it affected their family, the whole time looking up at the baby blue sky, rocking back and forth on his heels. When he was through, he looked over at me, calm and refreshed.

"I'm Paul."

"Eric." I stuck out my hand.

He grabbed it and looked me straight in the eye. "Thank you."

Paul puffed on the cancer stick one last time, dropped it on the ground, and stomped on it with his boot.

"Well, I've gotta get back to work." The bell on the door jingled as he went inside.

I've heard that every time a bell rings, an angel gets its wings. Maybe that was Paul's mother getting hers. I hope so. Her story certainly saved me. This walk was about people and how they've been affected by cancer: people like Paul and his mother, people like Austin Staples, people like the patients and caregivers I met at Massey Cancer Center. Their strength and courage was inspiring.

My golden friend in the sky wasn't about to quit for the day and neither was I. There were still miles to be made. Heavy swamp bracketed the highway that I was following. Every now and again, a car would whiz by or I'd pass a road sign. One in particular made me a little nervous about camping out that night. It said, "Unlawful To Feed Bears Along Highways." I kept wondering, "If a bear ate me, or a portion of me, would I be breaking the law?" The notion was ridiculous. Surely that bear would've been charged before me.

It was getting dark, so I started looking for a place to set up camp. The Dismal Swamp didn't provide many options. Finally, I discovered a paved road that was overgrown with weeds. They were creeping and causing cracks in the pavement like a very slow natural disaster. A sign on the gate said:

NO TRESPASSING, PRIVATE PROPERTY

The place looked as if it hadn't seen any action in years. I decided to break the law, with or without a bear, and nest a few hundred feet from the highway to hide the obvious blue and yellow colors of my tent. Camping out posed another challenge—dealing with Mother Nature.

The first night was colder than I expected. I could feel every sore bone, muscle, and tendon in my body. Shivering, I climbed into my tent, trying to evade the cutting wind. I garnered enough strength to remove my boots, which were stained with sea salt. As I carefully wrenched them off, I discovered my socks were saturated with blood. Some of it had already dried, making my socks difficult to peel from my raw skin. It was the kind of teeth-gritting pain that makes your eyes roll back in your head.

My feet were covered with bulging, fluid-filled sacs and bloody holes. I had to play both nurse and patient, draining the blisters, swabbing the open wounds with alcohol, and using an extra shirt to cover my mouth as I screamed in pain.

When I was through, I exhaled. I could see my breath. The sun had disappeared and my world was a shadow. I was wearing every piece of clothing I had, and still my body constantly quaked. I even slipped the bottom half of my body into my pack, but it didn't help. For some reason, I thought the weather was going to be warmer, so I hadn't brought a sleeping bag.

Under these conditions, I convinced myself I was either going to

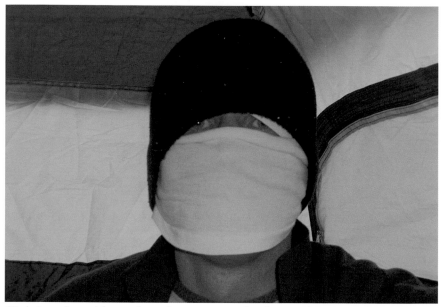

Fighting the cold weather: Camping on the first night in North Carolina.

freeze to death or get up and start moving. Despite objections from my feet, I packed up my gear and began marching down the dark and narrow highway.

It was a bad idea from the start. My blood was flowing again, but my legs were dragging. My flashlight was going dead. The highway was pitch black, and I was all alone. No vehicles had passed for at least a half an hour.

Just then, I noticed some headlights in the distance. It was a truck. All of a sudden, the purr of its engine died. It slowed down and pulled off the side of the road about a hundred yards ahead of me. When the driver killed the headlights, I stopped dead in my tracks. Terrible thoughts began running through my head. I'd seen a million movies before, and this scene was straight out of a cheap "slasher" flick.

All in one motion, I turned off my flashlight and froze. It was a standoff, just me and whoever was driving the truck. I needed a diversion, maybe a bear. I thought about heading into the swamp, but as bad as it looked during the day, I could only imagine how fun it would've be at night. I was scared. Stupid "slasher" movies.

My attention remained locked on the truck until I heard a siren. When I turned around a police car was pulling up beside me. The passenger side window rolled down, and a man in uniform leaned over the seat.

"Hey, you ok?" he asked.

"Sort of." I paused and decided against the whole "tough-guy" routine. "No, not really."

"Whatcha doin' out here?" It was part of his job to ask questions.

I told the officer about the whole campaign, but he wasn't impressed. He took a quick glance at my pack.

"Well, you need to find a place to camp for the night. There's a turn-off about a mile ahead on the right."

"Yes sir, but I need your help." I've found that those are the magic words when it comes to law enforcement. He sat up swiftly and leaned forward with super hero attentiveness as I explained how he could be of assistance.

"You see that truck up there?"

The officer made visual confirmation and nodded.

"Would you mind escorting me past it?"

His expression switched from a perked sense of curiosity to puzzlement, but he was through asking questions.

"Sure, no problem," he said.

He drove beside me at a nice walking pace, about four miles an hour. As we passed the truck, I battled the urge to look at the driver. I turned only to see the police cruiser making a u-turn and pulling up behind the truck. I walked another hundred feet and watched from the side of the road. I could feel my blood pressure rise as the deputy approached the truck. That couldn't be good. Something bad always happens to cops in "slasher" flicks, but eventually both vehicles started up and they drove away slowly. I let out a deep breath that had been hiding in my lower lungs.

The "pull-off" wasn't quite a mile down the road. It was an entrance to something, blocked by a gate. I followed a fence around the property and set up camp behind some bushes. It had gotten even colder, but that didn't matter. I was completely sapped.

Until then, I never knew what it meant to be truly exhausted. Still, I managed a smile as I laid down and closed my eyes that night. I had gone 13 miles, which was the farthest I'd ever walked in day. Every great journey begins with a single step, and I'd taken it.

The wind shook my tent relentlessly that night, but I dreamt hard anyway. Under gray skies I packed up my gear the next morning and cringed as I took my first few steps. The tin man was going to need a little oil. A packet of energy gel would have to do. As I headed back toward the highway, I noticed an old rusty sign on the gate. It said, "East Lake Landfill."

Sleeping next to a landfill explained the raunchy stench in the air. Then again, I probably didn't smell like roses either. East Lake was my stop for the second day, so I was ahead of schedule. I'd learn that several factors would affect how far I could actually walk in a day: terrain, weather, interviews with people affected by cancer, meal breaks, bathroom breaks, speaking with the media, etc. You'd never know when something was going to come up. I had to stop several times that day to fix my feet. Besides fresh, dry socks, medical supplies were among the most precious commodities.

The Alligator Bridge looked harmless, and on most days it probably was. There wasn't much room for pedestrians. I was within an arm's distance of cars and large trucks that would pass. They'd honk their horns at me. I tried to smile and wave, but a bully wind was shoving me back and forth. Every time a vehicle passed, I'd grab the side rail. My pack was ready to sail, nearly tossing me over the edge. The river was hungry. Like teeth, razor sharp whitecaps waited to devour anything that fell victim. That included walkers.

Walking onto the Alligator Bridge near East Lake, North Carolina.

As I battled my way across, an older man with white hair and a matching moustache appeared outside the bridge building. He started waving his arms at me, yelling something. I couldn't understand him through the wind. I was sure that he was going to scold me for being out there. I staggered toward him. Rather than wasting another breath, he motioned me to follow him through a doorway. He slammed the heavy steel door behind us and secured the latch. For now, I was safe from the vicious grips of the 'Gator.'

The vault creaked and groaned like an old ship. The man who'd come to my rescue faced me with a grand smile. He took the pleasure of introducing both of us.

"Hey, I'm Pete Gottfried, and you're one crazy bastard."

"I've been told that a lot lately," I said after laughing.

Pete wasn't from the Carolina's. Maybe Pittsburgh. He wore a Steelers sweatshirt. His accent hailed from somewhere above the Mason-Dixon line, but it didn't keep him from treating me with southern hospitality.

"Art and I just figured you might like a break," he said.

I'd never met Art, but I already liked the guy. A break sounded great. After wrestling with the wind, I felt like I had been run over by a truck. With Pete's approval, I left my gear near the steel door. He led me up a rusty spiral staircase. I had a feeling Art would be waiting at the top. We entered a small room. Only a couple of people could fit, maybe three. Windows covered one of the walls, making for a great view. A man stood, gazing into the murky water, his thoughts safe at the bottom. He surfaced at the clanking of our shoes on the staircase. It was Art.

We all sat down and he handed me a cup of water from the cooler. I chugged it, and he started filling it up again.

"So, where ya going?" Art asked.

He handed me the first refill. I chugged it before saying a word. He chuckled and looked at Pete.

"San Francisco," I said out of breath, "I'm walking ocean to ocean to raise money for cancer research."

Art filled up the cup one more time and handed it back to me. He and Pete were about the same age, mid to late 50's. They were bridge operators. Pete was training Art how to open and close the gate to let boats through, but there weren't any boats passing on that day. The gate was closed to any water traffic because of the weather. Pete pointed at the wind gauge on the wall.

"It's been blowing steady at 40 miles an hour with gusts up to 54," he said.

Pete and Art at Alligator Bridge Control in North Carolina.

Art shook his head and added, "It's pretty nasty out there."

All three of us looked out over the water. Before leaving, Pete asked if I was going through Roper. I nodded. That was my scheduled stop the third day.

Pete went on, "Well, you're welcome to stay with me and my wife Sunshine. She's a cancer survivor and she'd love to meet you."

I erupted, "Are you kidding me? That would be great!"

Pete and Sunshine were waiting for me when I arrived in Roper a couple of days later. Dinner was already in the oven, and wonderful smells lingered throughout the house.

"Sorry we don't have any pickled beets and eggs," said Sunshine with an omniscient smile. Somehow she knew PB&E was one of my favorites. They'd been on the campaign web site.

I shoved a fork-full of some kind of cheesy casserole in my mouth and smiled at them. They smiled back approvingly like parents do. Pete and Sunshine made me feel like family, like a son who'd been away for too long.

Sunshine wasn't your typical middle-aged woman. It was a miracle that she was even sitting at the table. Twenty-six years earlier she'd been diagnosed with cervical cancer. Doctors only gave her six to nine months to live, but that's not the miracle. Over the years, she

Sunshine and Pete at their home in Roper, North Carolina.

struggled with diabetes, narcolepsy, and even had two heart attacks. And she still kept a nice home.

Sunshine went above and beyond the call of duty. Being a registered nurse, she asked to look at my feet. I pulled off my size 15's with a grimace. The fresh blood sent her into concerned mother mode, but I didn't want to be a burden.

"It's not as bad as it looks," I explained. Sunshine knew better.

"We're going to soak your feet," she said. It didn't seem right that this wonderful woman, who'd had two heart attacks, was waiting on me hand and foot.

"You don't have to do that," I resisted.

"I know I don't have to," she said sternly, yielding to a warm smile, " I want to." In this world there are givers and takers. Sunshine was definitely a caregiver. We soaked my feet in warm, soapy water that night and put salve on them to control the infection.

The next morning, I hobbled into the dining room to find Pete sitting at the table.

"You should be on there," he pointed to the TV.

I laughed and shook my head. "They're not interested. I just started, and I've got a long way to go."

"You'll make it," he encouraged me. "You just have to keep going, no matter what."

I could tell Pete had been through a lot. He'd lost his mother to

Sunshine and Pete on their bikes.

cancer and been there for Sunshine through some of the most difficult times. When I asked what kept them going, Pete said, "We get
a kick out of life."

"Sunshine, what keeps you going?" I asked.

With a wry smile, she stuck her thumb at Pete and said, "He does."

Sunshine convinced me to stay an extra day to rest my feet, but
it wasn't just a quiet Sunday of reflection. After showing me their
personal motorcycles, we spent the afternoon at the Outer Banks
Speedway. We even managed to raise $44 for cancer research.

It was hard to leave Pete and Sunshine. I was a complete
stranger, and they invited me into their home. They fed me, they
fixed up my feet, and most importantly, they believed in me at a time
when I needed it most. Right before I left, Pete gave me a Pittsburgh
Pirates hat to protect my face from the sun.

The sun was setting as I walked into Lewiston. It had been
another long day, and I was ready to sleep. I asked a few people if
they knew of a safe place to camp, but two of them wouldn't speak
with me, and the third told me to keep walking. So I did. I walked
into town and stopped at the volunteer fire station. A woman
walked out of a house across from it, slamming the screen door. I

was sitting on the gravel parking lot with my back up against the building. She looked at me, and I smiled.

"What're you doin' out here?" She asked.

"Just resting," I said.

"Oh. Well, I'm Aunt Tis-Is," she said with one of the most cordial smiles I'd ever seen. When I told her about the walk, she invited me in for dinner and introduced me to her brother, Joseph. Joseph wasn't exactly thrilled that I was in his house. His sister brought home a tall, lanky white guy, who could have been homeless for all he knew. Joseph looked at me and then his sister.

"He's walking cross the country for cancer research," she said.

Joseph and Aunt Tis-Is in Lewiston, North Carolina.

Aunt Tis-Is grabbed my hand and led me into the kitchen. I sat at the dinner table, opposite a small TV and watched a preacher literally sweat his faith. Aunt Tis-Is believed in God and thought that everyone else should, too. After fixing some food, she sat next to me and held a conversation for both of us while I gobbled down a bowl of navy beans and ham.

"Where you staying tonight?" She asked.

"I'm looking for a place to camp."

"Camp in our yard," she said, assuming Joseph would be ok with it.

After dinner, I started setting up my tent in their front yard.

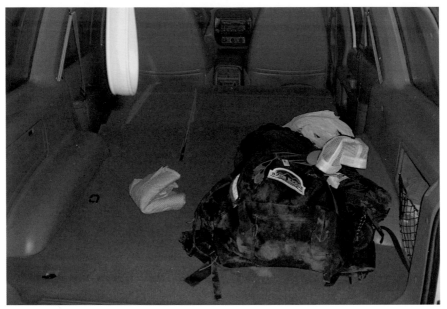

Sleeping in the back of Joseph Cherry's Mercury Mountaineer in Lewiston, North Carolina.

Then Joseph walked outside. When he didn't return my smile, I thought he was going to make me leave.

"That tent warm enough?" He asked.

"Yeah, it's pretty good," I said.

"If you want to," he said taking in a deep breath, " You could sleep in the back of our Mercury Mountaineer. It might be warmer."

It sounded like a strange idea, but Joseph wanted to help, so I accepted his kind gesture and slept pretty well.

North Carolina was a state of many firsts for me. Just outside of Kelford, there was a young woman walking on the opposite side of the road.

"Hello," I said.

"Hi," she said. "What're you doing?"

"Walking across the country for cancer research," I said, "What are you doin'?"

"Walking to my friends house." She crossed the road. "Mind if I walk with you?"

"That'd be great!" I said excitedly.

"I'm Edith Parker, but people call me E-low."

"I'm Eric Latham. People just call me Eric."

My First Walking Companion, Edith Parker (E-low) near Kelford, North Carolina.

E-low delivered a courtesy smile. She was the first person to walk with me. It was nice to have company and having conversation made the miles go by much quicker. During our walk, E-low told me about her friend Derick, who passed away because of lung cancer.

On my way to Pleasant Hill, I tried to take a shortcut, but got stuck in some swamps. Instead of turning around, I thought I'd just push through. That was a big mistake. Large splashes in the stagnant water not too far away made me wonder whether there were gators in the area. My arms and face were bloody from the thorn bushes, which were getting thicker.

When I finally found an opening in the brush, a brown snake hiding in the grass snapped at me and coiled up in attack position, ready to strike. By then, I was so irritated that I would've bitten back.

The opening was man-made. I could see several towers in the distance, which led me to believe I'd walked into a hunting area. It was a maze, and I couldn't find my way out. I tried every direction, but it was no use. I was lost. The beaming sun and lack of water made me a little paranoid. What if I was being hunted? It didn't matter. I was going to die out there anyway.

After stopping to change my bandages, I decided to try getting

Stuck in the North Carolina swamps.

out of there one last time. There was a way I hadn't tried yet. It was overgrown with brush, but I pushed my way through more pricker bushes to some open farmland.

I managed to stagger down a dirt road for a while. Finally, I saw a farmhouse in the distance. My stomach cringed as I gasped for water. I hadn't had any for hours. There was a small black truck in the driveway. I walked over to the house and up the wooden porch steps. My hand shook as I rang the doorbell. Nobody came. I rang the doorbell again and knocked. I thought that maybe the doorbell wasn't working. I positioned my ear close to the wooden door, but I couldn't hear anything.

Nearly tumbling down the porch steps, I collapsed on the front yard where I had dropped my pack. I waited for about ten minutes. I thought that maybe someone would come home, but nobody did. I couldn't go any further. One way or another, I was going to get water from that house, even if I had to break into it.

First, I'd search the perimeter for a water faucet. Four sides, four chances. There was nothing on the front of the house, nothing on the first side, and nothing in the back. My chances were fading quickly. I started thinking about how I would get into the house, but I still had one more side to try. I paused before turning the corner. Slowly, I took two steps forward and turned my head slightly to the left, a quivering smile growing on my face. With wild eyes I rushed over to the water faucet and cranked the creaky metal knob with my shaky hand. I positioned my head under the cold stream, choking on the water. After 20 seconds I flopped on the soft green grass, my lungs pumping hard. The clear baby blue sky was more beautiful than ever.

Garnering strength, I filled my water bottles and headed down the slightly sloping gravel driveway. It connected to a paved road. Where it came from or where it was going, I had no idea, so I just took a left. Not knowing how far I was from Pleasant Hill, I decided to look for a safe place to camp. A few miles down the road, there was another large farmhouse.

I walked up to a man working in the driveway.

"Hello there," I said.

"Yep?" He kept working.

"I'm walking across the country for cancer research, and I was wondering if I could camp in your yard?"

Vernie Davenport at her home in Garysburg, North Carolina.

"Couldn't tell ya. You'll have to ask the Davenports," he said pointing to the house, "This is their place."

Not knowing what to say, over a minute passed before I tapped my fist on the side of the screen door. An older woman approached the glass. She was wearing a vintage polyester button-up blouse and an apron. I smiled and waved nervously.

"Are you Mrs. Davenport?" I asked as polite as possible. Mrs. Davenport wore her hair the same way she had for many years.

"May I help you?" she asked in the sweetest southern drawl. I felt like a salesman.

"Hello, my name's Eric Latham. I'm walking from ocean to ocean for cancer research. I was wondering if y'all would mind if I camped in your yard for safety reasons."

It may have been too much all at once. She looked at me as though I was speaking another language.

"I'll have to call my sons," she said. I was sure they'd tell her no, but she returned after a few minutes and said it would be ok. After

I set up my tent, Mrs. Davenport brought me some ham sandwiches, snack cakes, and a couple of cold drinks.

Wind and rain rocked my tent all night long making for a bumpy ride through dreamland. I was up early and so was Mrs. Davenport. She'd prepared breakfast and brought it to me on a paper plate.

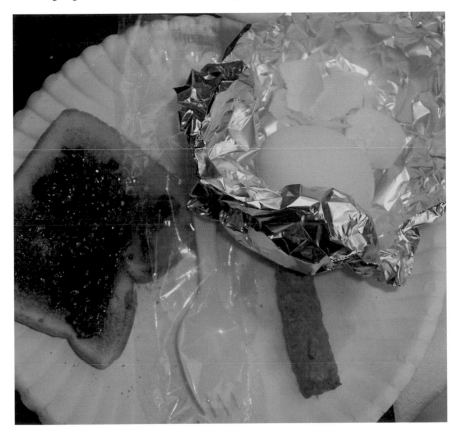

It was just what I needed to start the day. After packing up my gear, I dragged my heavy backpack to the door and knocked like an old friend. Mrs. Davenport came outside.

"I'm so glad I got to meet you," she said.

"Thanks for letting me stay here," I said. "You saved me." We both smiled and enjoyed a brief moment. Her smile expired first.

"You know, my husband's got cancer," she said trying not to cry.

I didn't know what to say, so I just hugged her. In less than 24 hours, we'd become good friends, and I'd probably never see her again. Before heading down the road, I handed Mrs. Davenport a card and told her to call me anytime.

When I reached the border of Virginia, I threw my hands in the air and screamed. Some guys working on the railroad next to the highway were staring at me, but I didn't care. All my emotions formed a lump at the back of my throat. The physical and mental stresses were beginning to mount. My walk through North Carolina was the most challenging thing I'd ever done. It felt amazing, but I still had 11 states and thousands of miles to go. The big picture was overwhelming.

CHAPTER 2

Old Dominion

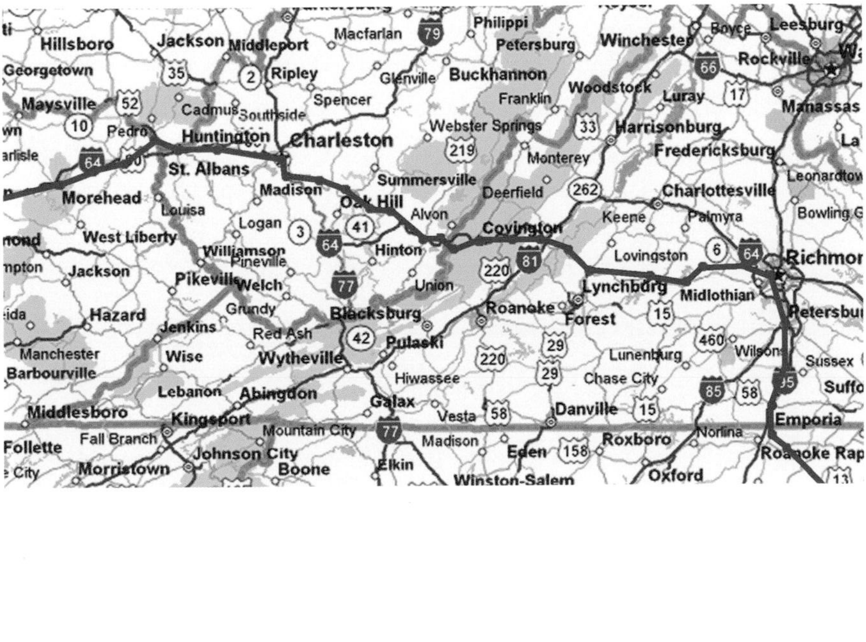

Their pitted skin crawled as drool dripped from their snarling lips. It was either them or me, and all I could think was that I should've taken the gun I'd been offered. From the moment they laid their bloodshot eyes on me, they could tell I was scared. I wore fear like some cheap eau de toilette, and they hated it.

With each vicious bark, they could nearly taste the sinews of my flesh. I imagined they'd go for the jugular or start by tearing off each of my limbs from their sockets, devour the mess, and bury my bones for a rainy day. That looked like the end of the road for our walker. I was about to be mauled by two mangy mutts, but I decided that wasn't good enough.

Quickly, out of my side bag, I pulled some crusty hamburger buns that I'd been given along the way. I jingled the bag high above my head to divert their deadly intentions and tossed it into the woods. Hook, line, and sinker. They ran after the bag, I scurried by, and that's how my buns saved me.

~

Walking into a new town each day, being a stranger all over again, made things difficult. My purpose was not greatly known, and proving to people that I wasn't just some vagrant practicing civil degeneracy was, from time to time, a sour sociological lesson. Alienation was setting in like some rare festering disease, chewing on my conscience, and spitting out any kind of rationality.

Emporia was larger than most towns I'd walked through so far. People were popping in and out of shops, boutiques, and salons that lined historic Main Street. The gray cement sidewalks were worn. I greeted many wandering sets of eyes with a gentle smile, hoping to diffuse any concern for my being. Some people were friendly. Others ignored me.

The local hardware store caught my attention. Through the large glass storefront window, I could see four men having a conversation. I pushed open the door and walked up to them.

Emporia, Virginia.

"So, this is Emporia," I said, "What's it known for?" The men just stared at me. I was just about to turn around and leave when one of them, who was wearing denim bibbed overalls and a flannel shirt, spoke up.

"Pork and peanuts," he said with a hearty laugh. "That's 'bout it."

Another one said. "Yep, not like it used to be." After that, I was just one of the boys, and they told me everything I wanted to know about Emporia.

Asking people about their towns was a great conversation starter. They either knew something or they didn't, but they'd always ask about my shirt. Then I'd tell them about the walk, and they'd tell me what they knew about cancer. Stores were a good place to meet people but local restaurants or diners were better.

There was only one place to eat in Stony Creek. Carter's 1 Stop was quaint, and it hadn't changed for at least 20 years. The family-owned joint was empty when I walked in. The waitress greeted me after I took a seat at one of the yellow and brown booths. She stood waiting with her pen and pad while I glanced up and down the menu.

"The special's meat loaf, mashed potatoes, green beans, and your choice of coffee or sweet tea," she said.

"Sounds good. I'll have the tea."

Before long, the dinner crowd filed in. A medium-sized man with a buzz cut sat down at a booth in front of me.

"Cancer Research Walker," he said in a raspy, almost electronic voice. Luke Irby insisted on buying me dinner after I told him about the walk. Nearly a year before I met him, Luke was diagnosed with cancer in his throat. He had to drive to Massey Cancer Center (where I volunteered) in Richmond, every day for seven weeks straight to receive radiation treatments, affecting the way his voice sounded.

Luke pointed to his mouth. "And now my taste buds and salivary glands don't work," he said shaking more salt on his food. "Can't taste a damn thing."

After losing both parents to cancer, Luke didn't want anyone to go through what he had. If he had to live with cancer, the cancer would have to live with him. Luke wasn't afraid to talk about it. He owned his cancer, which gave him a greater appreciation for life.

"Some people give up," he stopped and started in a more serious tone, "But not me."

Luke Irby at Carter's 1 Stop in Stony Creek, Virginia.

After we finished eating, Luke motioned for me to come sit next to him, and our conversation shifted gears.

"You ever get scared?" He asked.

I answered his question with another.

"You mean on the walk?"

He nodded.

"Sometimes," I said.

Slowly, Luke reached into his pocket and pulled out a shiny black pistol, using the table to hide it from any curious sets of eyes.

He leaned closer. "Wanna take some protection?"

My heart skipped a beat. I wondered if it was loaded. Quickly, I shook my head.

"No thanks," I said.

In a very nonchalant way, Luke tilted his head, shrugged, and placed the pistol back in his pocket. Cool Hand Luke.

Even considering carrying a gun just didn't seem right. I could see the headlines, "Cancer Research Walker Turns Gun-Toting Thug." But Luke meant well, just like the rest of the people I met at Carter's 1 Stop.

As one woman put it, "We're a tight-knit community with a lot of love to give."

One of the Carters said I could set up camp in a wooded area only a stone's throw from their building. It was close enough for safety and far enough to avoid a possible confrontation.

I set up the tent suite just before dark. My one-man tent was quite small, actually. I had to lie diagonally in it just to fit. That night in Stony Creek was the first time I really encountered wild animals. Curious critters would graze the tent, rubbing against my head and feet, which were pushing on opposite corners of the delicate nylon structure. Then I'd wake up to hear them rattling around and rummaging outside. I got used to it, but I could only imagine (and even relish) how it might scare the heck out of my four sisters.

Two of them, Angie and Caitlin, joined me for the walk into Richmond. After several hours and about 11 miles, they were ready to call it a day. One of my other sisters, Kleo, came to pick them up, and I kept walking.

I'd only been away for a week and a half, but somehow Richmond looked different. I spent the next day volunteering at Massey Cancer Center. It was great to be back until another volunteer said something that made my blood boil. I was telling some people about the walk so far, when he asked, "How do we know you haven't been just sitting at home, making it all up?" He looked at the other people in the room as if he was pleading his case to a jury.

My sisters Caitlin and Angie between Petersburg and Richmond, Virginia.

My heart sunk. I wanted to slug him. Instead, I laughed it off and hid behind a diplomatic smile. Still, it made me wonder why anything I was doing really mattered. I wasn't walking to prove the skeptics wrong. I was walking to prove the believers right.

Before leaving MCC, I decided to weigh myself. When I created Walk About America in September 2004, I weighed 205 pounds. When I started walking, I weighed 188 pounds. When I weighed myself that day, I was only 179 pounds!

On my last night in Richmond, I participated in the American Cancer Society's annual Bachelor Auction fundraiser. Bachelor Auctions can be shameful events. You stand there under a spotlight, terrified, while hundreds of women bid on you like a piece of meat. I loved every minute of it.

A nice lady bought me for $150, which was a steal if you ask me, but the whole thing really wasn't fair to her. I was supposed to take her on a date, but I had to start walking again the next day. It was hard to fathom having any kind of relationship during the walk. Angie always joked that I'd be walking in Minnesota, fall in love with some farm girl, and forget about the whole campaign.

I'd only been away for ten days when I walked into Richmond. It was like being on vacation, so when my time there was over, I knew the real journey was about to begin. Kleo and one of her

Dressed up for the ACS Bachelors Auction in Richmond, Virginia.

friends walked with me to Manakin. When we got there, I couldn't celebrate with them. They headed back to Richmond, and I kept going, but at least I wasn't completely alone. More and more people were stopping to talk.

Roy Palmer, Sr. began to cry when he pulled up in his car. His son, Roy Jr., who battled cancer, had died in a motorcycle accident recently.

"I had to bury my son," he said, choked up on tears.

Roy Palmer, Sr. near Manakin, Virginia.

Roy gathered himself and shook my hand before driving away. I've always had a difficult time showing my emotions, but hearing devastating stories every day was starting to take its toll. For so many years, a barrier controlled and contained all my feelings. That barrier was breaking down, and meeting Roy put me over the edge.

By then, I was developing a routine before going to bed each night: clean and re-bandage my feet, eat a snack (usually an energy bar and a little water), update the campaign web site, and review my route for the next day. And almost every night, I'd read a letter from my mother. It included a poem she'd written for my little brother, Michael, who died way before his time. Ma said my middle name, Michael, was given to me after him or along with him, "Certainly like brothers, the name connecting you," she wrote. Lonely and hoping that he could hear me, I'd lay in my tent and read Ma's words out loud:

"Michael"

You were special, a dream come true,
The last little Latham.
But you were sick.
Your dad asked you, "do you want to live?"
You replied, "for awhile."
We were glad.
You lived almost a year; it seemed like a lifetime,
It was.
You touched those who met you with your strength
To fight, your will to live.
You touched many who never met you but just
Heard of you.
You gave us strength, for how could we falter
When you endured so much.
There were times when you were a happy and
Content baby—
Those memories will never fade.
You knew each brother and sister and loved each one.
They loved you more than anything,
You were their Mygoo.
At your bed I held your hand—it was still warm—
I was glad.
I laid my head near you & you had a special smell.
Near the end, when I would put your hand down
You would peek at me.
"Mom, where are you going?"
Michael forgive me for numbing myself to the pain you endured.
I was selfish, I wanted you.
You touched the hearts of those who knew you
With your sweet angel face.
Life will never be the same.
Mostly, I feared the hospital, you were sick.
Then I learned to love the hospital, you were there.

I used to rush there to be with you.
I rushed home; I always stayed too long.
Now there's no place to rush to.
There's peace for you, quiet, a void for me.
I feel empty inside and lonely.
My heart aches for you and we miss you so.
Help me fill that void with love for others.
You are so special Michael.
Your life was not in vain.
You were loved so very, very much.
Good night for now Sweet Michael.
Love Mom
July 1985

I'm not a crying man, but every time I read that poem, tears streamed down my face. It was about Michael. It was about being lonely. It was about the people I was meeting and the difficult journey I was facing. And mostly, it was about holding it in for so many years and just letting go. We all have different ways of dealing with our past. As painful as it may be, sometimes we have to confront it in order to accept it.

Gaining elevation: 887 feet above sea level outside of Amherst, Virginia.

The thought of walking 32 miles in a day didn't help. That's how far it was to Amherst. And the terrain was changing. I'd reached the foothills of the Appalachian Mountains. Surprisingly, it was easier walking up a hill than down it. The descent was harder on my joints. My hips would pop, and I could always feel the raw spots on my feet, which felt as though I was rubbing off another layer of skin with each step. By the time I reached Amherst, I'd walked 338 miles.

George Washington National Forest near Buena Vista, Virginia.

On my way to Lexington, I studied my maps and decided that it would be easier to get there by walking on Interstate 81. I made it a few miles before a state trooper pulled me over. By then, I'd learned to step away from my bags and keep my hands in clear view.

"What're you doing?" Asked the officer.

"Walking across the country for cancer research."

"Not on this interstate," he said pointing to the passenger side of his cruiser, "Get in."

It was clear that I didn't have a choice. He was talking to me like a criminal, and I'd done nothing wrong. The officer drove me back a couple miles and dropped me off on a side road. Before getting out, he told me that he should've given me a summons. All I could think was, "Well, you know where I'll be."

The sun was setting as I walked through the very small community of Crows, right on the border of Virginia and West Virginia. I set up my tent about 25 yards off the rural route I was following. Using my flashlight, I began working on my feet.

The natural sounds of the forest were in full harmony. Birds were singing and crickets were chirping. All of a sudden, it went dead quiet. Puzzled, I looked up and listened closely, lifting the wool hat covering my ears. I turned off my flashlight and waited. Then I heard it.

"Tromp! Tromp! Tromp! Tromp! Tromp!"

Something had walked right up to the side of the tent about a foot in front of me. I tried to sit very still, hoping it wouldn't know I was there. On top of the tent suite, about four inches from my head, there was a vent that let fresh air in. Whatever it was, leaned over the top of the tent, and began to sniff. A cold chill went up my spine. I was about to be eaten.

When it stopped sniffing, I sat in silence for 10–15 seconds, which seemed like an hour.

"Tromp! Tromp! Tromp! Tromp! Tromp!"

It took off. I never found out what it was. Maybe it was a good thing that I hadn't bathed in a few days.

CHAPTER 3

The Mountain State

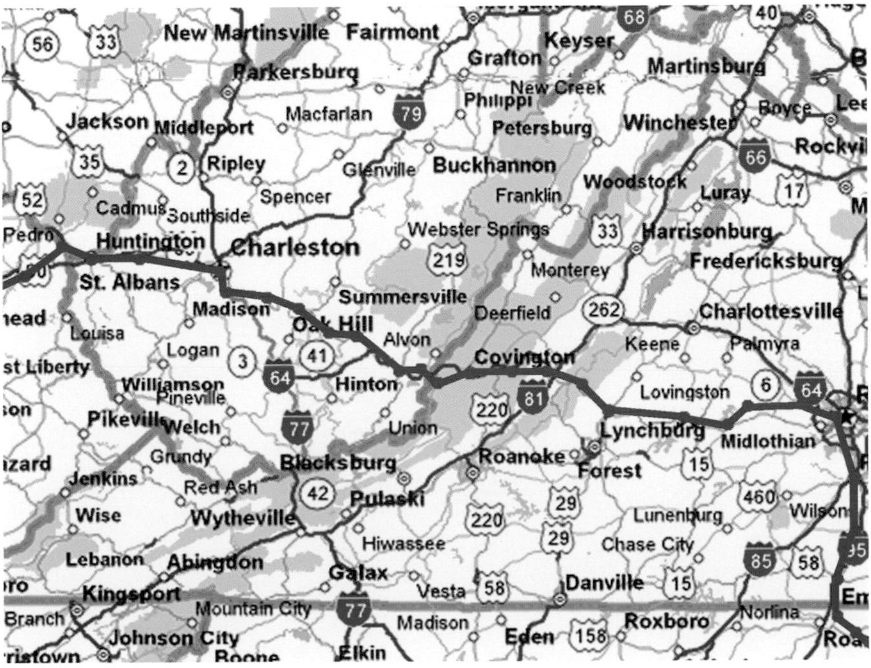

It was a constant reminder, the sharp pain in my shoulders. Carrying a 60-pound pack across the country was like giving a large child a very long piggyback ride. But almost everything it contained was necessary in conducting a safe and successful campaign. I carried a laptop computer, a sleeping bag (which I picked up in Richmond), the tent suite, water, medical supplies, fresh socks, maps, and an odd assortment of items that people had given me along the way. I called it the, "Here, I want you to take this with you" phenomenon. Many times they were sentimental items, like a four-foot tall teddy bear or a lucky barbell set (Ok, so it wasn't always that ridiculous).

Most people had good intentions, like Nathan King in Montgomery, West Virginia. When I walked into town, I smelled a barbeque. At first, I thought my mind was playing tricks on me, but then I noticed some people grilling outside a house. That's how I met Nathan and his family.

Nathan King (gray shirt) and his family in Montgomery, West Virginia.

We started talking about the walk and they invited me up on their porch to partake in the barbeque festivities. Nathan was a family man, and I could tell he enjoyed helping people. He took it upon himself to make sure that I got enough to eat, and he succeeded. I ate like a "King," literally. The King's made me feel at home, like I was just part of the family.

Before leaving, Nathan pointed to the grill and insisted that I take some food with me. I was stuffed, so I expressed my concern that the food would spoil if I didn't eat it soon. In a flash, he ran into the house, and returned with a bag. It was full of canned goods, about 20 pounds worth.

"This should last you for a while," he said with a big smile. Nathan wasn't going to take no for an answer, and I wasn't going to refuse his kindness. I needed help. It was the only way I'd make it across the country.

❧

I'd meet some of the nicest people in West Virginia, where the mountains seemed to be alive, green and growing. I truly understood the state license plate slogan: West Virginia, Wild and Wonderful.

At over 3,000 feet above sea level, Hilton Village was one of the highest points I crossed on the east coast. The campground there was closed, but since I had no other place to stay, I decided to camp there anyway. Around sundown, three younger guys started walking toward my tent. One of them was wearing a camouflage jacket.

Popping out of my tent with a smile, I wanted to make sure they knew I wasn't a threat. Still, they approached cautiously. One of the guys introduced himself as the owner of the campground. The other two guys were his friends. The owner said it was ok that I was camping there, but they just wanted to make sure I wasn't some "weirdo." After telling them some stories about the walk, they became interested. In fact, the guy in the camouflage jacket, Calvin Braggs, had lost his mother to cancer.

I asked Calvin what he remembered about this mother. His memories were limited, but one stood out.

"I remember watching her brush her hair… and it all falling out," he said. Tears were forming in Calvin's eyes as if he were experiencing the pain all over again. He continued anyway.

Calvin Braggs and I in Hilton Village, West Virginia.

"She was crying and I couldn't do a thing." Calvin's mother had been taking chemotherapy.

Before heading home, the guys asked me if I needed anything. They'd already given me a chance, helping restore my faith in humanity, and I thanked them for that.

A warm steady breeze was blowing through the park that evening. I sat in the soft, cool grass and examined the condition of my feet, which seemed to be improving. The constant bleeding had subsided and calluses were starting to form over the raw areas. The war on bacteria had ceased for the time being.

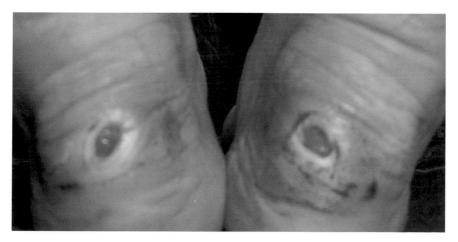

The Capitol Building on the Kanawha River in Charleston, West Virginia.

On my way out of Charleston, I stopped at a little café downtown and ordered the usual. Coffee. Black. No sugar. No Cream. No nothing. With each tongue-torching gulp of the scalding high-octane liquid, I could feel my body begin to come alive. We were back in business.

I took a seat at a small table and pulled out my laptop. Two women, lounging in a trendy, plush couch to my right, asked if I was the guy walking across the country. They'd recognized me from the morning paper. One of them held up the article, which included a picture of me walking. After speaking with them about the walk, they recommended that I visit the Charleston Area Medical Center, Women and Children's Hospital.

There were several children receiving treatment when I walked into the pediatric oncology unit. My heart sank. It was the exact feeling that I got when I saw Austin Staples in his hospital room. I kept thinking, "Children shouldn't have to go through that."

Curious, young eyes watched my yellow shirt as I took a tour of the pediatric unit. Then one of the nurses introduced me to Andrea, Abbigail, and Lois (Abbigail's Mam-ma).

Abbigail was only 17 months old at the time. She was battling neuro-blastoma, a rare form of childhood cancer. Andrea, her mother, said it had been a long journey.

Andrea, Abbigail, and Lois in Charleston, West Virginia

"Once she [Abbie] started losing her hair, we knew it was real."

Abbie was a beautiful child with baby blue eyes. Her light brown hair was trying to grow back. On the outside, she looked normal, but on the inside, something she couldn't understand was invading her body. While other kids her age were playing, she was at the hospital, dealing with an immense amount of pain.

"Would you like to hold her?" Andrea held up Abbie.

I took little Abbie into my arms and cradled her. When I looked into her eyes, my heart ached and my soul began to suffer. Her pain was my pain. It was like little Abbie and I were communicating on another level. Although she couldn't speak, her eyes said, "Help me. Help me."

Here she was, only 17 months old, fighting for her life. It made me angry seeing little Abbie like that, seeing all those kids like that. I wanted to turn over a table or break a chair on the wall. It wasn't fair.

Tears began to flow the moment I walked out of the hospital. I wasn't about to cry in front of Abbie, or her mom, or anybody. The pain on little Abbie's face was permanently sired into my memory. Her strength and courage inspired me. She gave me hope. She'd done so much for me that I wanted to do something to help her. If this campaign could make a difference for just one minute, it would mean an eternity to me.

Before saying goodbye, Andrea gave me a purple rubber bracelet with Abbie's full name on it. The 17-month-old miracle smiled when I placed it over my wrist. It was the first bracelet I was given but not the last. I found out later that little Abbie passed away on December 9, 2005, five days after her second birthday.

Chapter 4

The Bluegrass State

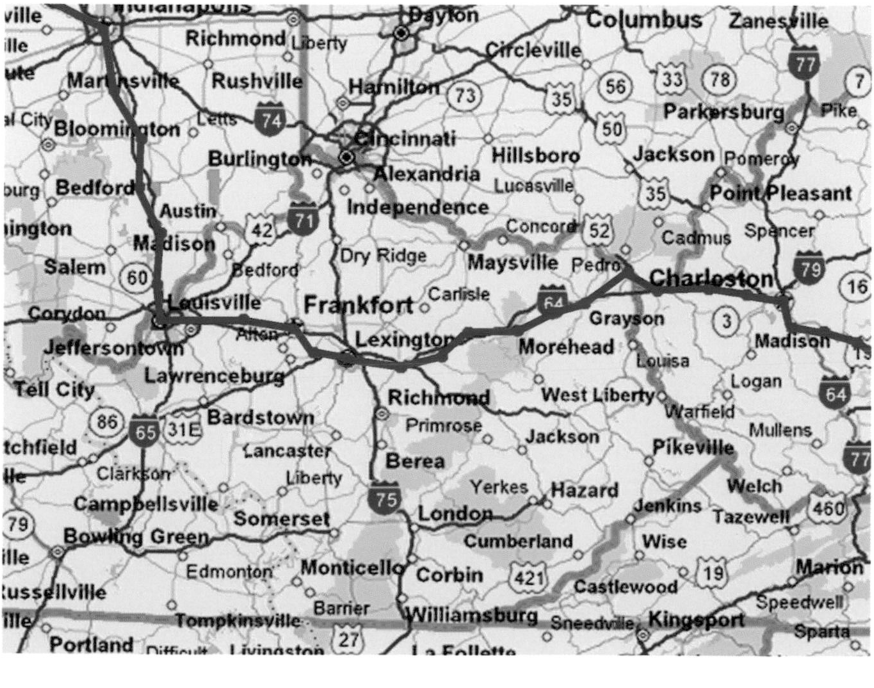

*L*ove's the greatest offender, yet shackled and bound are its victims. Maybe Aimee and I were victims, at least for a few moments. We stared at each other across the wooden table with the most ridiculous and uncontrollable smiles. A glass lamp, hanging above our green-cushioned booth, lit up her angel face. Outside, the sky was crying, but we laughed anyway. I mean, who serves cheap tap beer in glass flutes? Still, it helped wash down the mushroom and chicken pizza we shared.

Everything she said was important, from the day she was born, to the accident that killed her mother, to her college days, to San Francisco, to Louisville and a lot of glue in between. Aimee was complex and completely beautiful. It was hard to believe I wouldn't have even met her if she hadn't survived cancer.

∾

Louisville was my last stop in Kentucky. I'd already spent 13 days in the Bluegrass State, and thanks to one of my Delta Sigma Phi fraternity brothers and a journalist in Morehead, I didn't have to spend much time in the tent suite.

Just outside of Owingsville, I noticed something coming toward me in the grass on the other side of the highway. As it got closer, I realized it was a dog. I stopped to see if she was following me. She stopped, too. I started walking and stopped again when she came a little closer. She paused and watched for my next move. I scampered a few steps back toward her and she retreated. When I turned around and began walking, she started following me again. That's when I named her, "Shy."

I didn't want Shy to get hit by a car, so I stopped at a gas station and waited for her to catch up. At first, Shy wouldn't let me get within 20 feet of her. She wagged her tail nervously as I put my pack down.

"Shy" my canine for cancer research near Owingsville, Kentucky.

Not all dogs were out to get me. Shy and I became friends immediately. She was my "Canine for Cancer Research." I guessed Shy
was about six years old (that's about 42 in dog years). She poured
on her big brown puppy-dog eyes. I wanted to take her along, but I
knew I couldn't. I was having a hard enough time taking care of
myself. She probably already had a home anyway. After giving her
a thorough belly scratching, I patted her on the side.

"Can't go this time, girl."

Shy tilted her head and looked up at me as if she was confused.
I stood up and pointed.

"Now, go home." Shy began trotting away, looking back a few
times, maybe to see if I was following her.

Most of the time when people would stop their vehicles to share
their stories with me they'd smile and wave, but that wasn't the case
with Joe Vanderpool. Joe just sat there after pulling his truck over in
a deserted lot in front of me. All I could do was keep walking.

"You the walker?" he asked as I was passing the truck window.

"Yeah."

Joe proceeded to tell me the story of his mother-in-law who was
battling cancer. It was first diagnosed in her lungs and had since
spread to her liver, but the cancer was just more bad news for their

Joe Vanderpool in central Kentucky

family. One of her sons was murdered. Her granddaughter was bedridden after a horrible automobile accident, and her other son had a massive heart attack and died. Three months later, she was diagnosed with cancer.

A tear rolled down Joe's tired face as he finished speaking. About a minute later, he wiped his eyes and broke the silence.

"She's a tough woman."

I didn't know what to say, so I just nodded. We were complete strangers, but cancer brought us together. That's what it does. It forms a bond between people who don't even know each other or have nothing else in common. Cancer doesn't affect just one type of person. It's not specific to gender, age, race, ethnic background, religion, sexual orientation, or socio-economic status. It affects us all.

At first, I was hesitant about calling the American Cancer Society in Louisville, especially after my experience with them in Lexington. But ACS was a very important part of this campaign, so I decided to call them anyway. I'm glad I did.

From the sound of her voice, I assumed she was in her late 40's or 50's, but one thing was certain. Ms. Aimee Reed was an extremely helpful American Cancer Society representative. She worked in the public relations department. Our future relations, however, would not be immediately public.

Horse Farm near Frankfort, Kentucky.

How she did it, I'll never know. Maybe she was an expert, but Ms. Reed had set up interviews with two television stations, a radio station, and the local newspaper shortly after our phone conversation. All I could think was, "Damn, she's good."

The improvised press conference would take place at Applebee's. We were shooting for 3:30 p.m. I'd never been to that part of Kentucky, so it was difficult gauging how long it would take me to get there. Arriving a half an hour early, I laid my pack down and sat on the grass. The looks from the "coming and going" didn't bother me anymore.

It was nearing three and a half, so I was keeping an eye out for Ms. Reed. One of the employees and I were standing in front of the restaurant talking about the campaign, when a white Ford Escape pulled up. When a younger woman got out, I knew it couldn't be Ms. Reed. Ms. Reed was much older. This woman appeared to be in her twenties. Still, I couldn't take my eyes off her slender body and long blond hair. She looked at me and smiled, sending a shock through my soul. Certainly, this was just a kind person having a good day, probably meeting someone for happy hour or an early dinner. No, it wouldn't be that simple. Our eyes locked. I tried to be polite and arrest a growing grin. It was no use. She sauntered toward me and held out her hand.

"You must be the walker." It was the voice.

My jaw dropped. "Ms. Reed?"

"Aimee," she said.

I wanted to keep holding her delicate hand during the interviews, but I didn't even know this woman. Yet.

Man, Aimee was distracting. Her electrifying exuberance was making me crazy. I could hardly speak with the reporters and wondered if anything I said made sense. It didn't matter at that point. She was all I could think about.

I'd have to finish off my walk that day in the rain, which I didn't mind. Maybe it would cool me off a little. A journalist was supposed to meet me in town for dinner, but something had come up.

Aimee wasn't going to let me eat alone. She asked me what I wanted for dinner. When I told her that I was really craving pizza, we decided on the California Pizza Kitchen. It was hard to believe I wouldn't have even met her if she hadn't survived cancer.

Aimee had hardly considered the mole on her arm life threatening, but her dad asked her to get it checked anyway. After the biopsy, the doctor's directions were, "Call us if you don't hear anything within ten days." Ten days passed without a word, and she thought no news was good news. But when she made the call, they asked her to come back immediately.

The doctor pulled up a stool in front of Aimee and held her hands.

"You have cancer."

Aimee didn't know what to think or what it meant. Right then and there, she was diagnosed with melanoma, the deadliest form of skin cancer. Aimee couldn't believe it. She was only 25 years old. Two years later, she was sitting in front of me. Aimee pulled up her sleeve, revealing a four-inch scar from surgery. I wanted to collect her hands in mine and tell her everything was going to be ok.

After dinner, Aimee said she could drive me to my hotel, but somehow, we got lost. She missed the exit. Secretly, I didn't care. I wanted to spend as much time as I could with her. Eventually, we found the hotel and said good night. "See you soon" would have been more appropriate.

Aimee was back at the hotel early the next morning. When I got off the elevator, I could see her through the glass doors. Surely, I was dreaming. She'd set up a visit to Kosair Children's Hospital, but first, I had to get some walking done.

"Would you wear this?" Aimee held in the palm of her perfectly crafted hand a black, metal ribbon with the outline of a gold heart in it. I smiled and wanted to give her a big hug, but for some "big idiot" reason, I decided to play it cool.

"Sure, no problem." She pinned it at the top of my shirt. I was walking for Ms. Reed, for Aimee.

Aimee and I in Louisville, Kentucky.

At Kosair, it would have been difficult meeting all those sick children on my own, but I had Aimee by my side. We'd share the experience.

We were introduced to Andrew, an 11-year-old with a brain tumor. When we walked into his room it was clear that wrestling was his passion. Everything had a wrestling theme: figurines, championship belts, and posters.

"What about this one?" I asked about a poster of a female wrestler. Andrew just smiled. Immediately I thought about Austin Staples. Austin was just a kid with his whole life ahead of him, and Andrew was no different.

"If there's one thing I could do for you on this walk," I asked, "What would it be?"

Andrew thought about it for a second and looked down at my walking stick.

"You ever whacked anything with that?" He asked. We all laughed.

If there was something that rivaled Andrew's passion for wrestling, it was Big Red Soda. He loved it so much that he wanted to share it with me. Andrew insisted that I take a bottle from his private stash. He was so happy when I took a swig of it. Andrew had such an impact on me that I cut off the barcode from that bottle and carried it with me the rest of the way.

The extremely helpful ACS representative and I took our time exiting the hospital. It was like a game, staring at each other out of the corners of our eyes as not to give anything away. But every time we would burst into laughter. We couldn't contain ourselves.

As soon as we reached her Escape, our time together was up. I was walking out of Louisville, and we didn't know whether we'd ever see each other again. It seemed unfair. Trying to make it easier on both of us, I just started walking away. I had to rationalize my leaving Aimee in Louisville. As I was crossing the Second Street Bridge into Indiana, I discovered a card in my side bag. It read:

Eric,

I don't even know where to begin. First of all, thank you. Thank you for making the journey of a lifetime to fight for a cause that you believe in. You are such an inspiration to many. I am truly blessed that I got the opportunity to meet you, that somehow in this world full of people, our paths have crossed. Your smile could light up the darkest room. And your eyes reveal the treasures of your soul. What an awesome person you are. I was drawn to you at first glance. I've enjoyed every single second we've spent together, and it's so hard to watch you leave. But I'll be with you every step of the way. That's why I wanted you to wear my ribbon, so that I could go with you. And I'm just among a long list of others whose hearts you've sincerely touched. The wonderful thing is that you'll be with us, too. You've left a permanent mark that will never leave. I don't want to fight this, Eric. I don't want to make things hard on you, but I believe that if you feel something for another person, you should tell them. Who knows when you'd get the chance again. So, I want you to know that you'll be on my mind, in my heart, and in my prayers always. I'll be counting the days until September 20th. And I'll talk to you all along the way. You are INCREDIBLE!!

Love, Aimee
June 2, 2005

Louisville, Kentucky from the Second Street Bridge.

CHAPTER 5

The Hoosier State

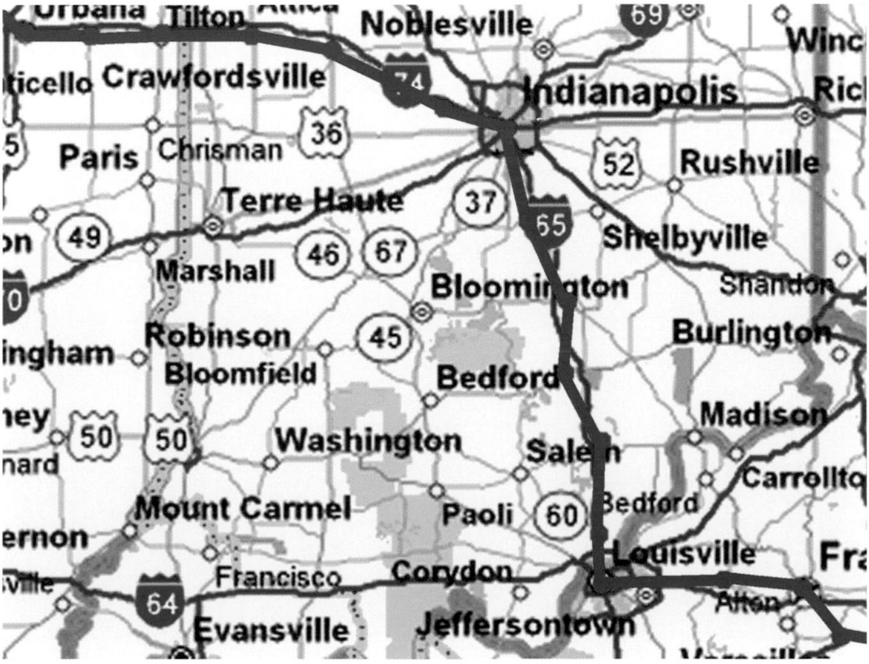

Many police officers wanted to give me a ride—right out of their town. They'd pull up and assume I was a trouble-maker. Usually after I told them about the campaign, they'd ask if I needed any help. One time on my way to Sellersburg a cruiser came to a screeching halt next to me.

"Have you been running through the cornfields?" The officer asked.

I looked around. "No."

We both knew it was an odd question, but he hoped that I was the key to some mystery. Out of curiosity, I prodded. "Why?"

"Well..." He didn't really want to tell me. "We got a report that someone was running through the cornfields...and fell flat on their face."

~

The smile on my face was a direct result of the conversation with Aimee. I had to call her after reading the card she stowed in my side bag. I finished crossing the Second Street Bridge into Indiana while speaking with her on my cell phone. There was something more between us, and we decided to try and figure it out that night.

A journalist had set up a hotel room for me in Clarksville and was driving up so we could have dinner. I called him when I arrived at the hotel, and he was a half an hour away. Aimee got there first. She drove to meet me right after work.

The rhythm of gentle tapping could have only been made by her delicate fists. I was nervous when I opened the door. Aimee stood there glowing, even more beautiful than I remembered. It had only been a few hours since we parted ways at Kosair.

She'd let her gorgeous golden locks down that night. I wanted to wrap my arms around her and never let go. Aimee was the kind of woman that made you want to throw all the rules out the window. It was like she and I were made for each other. So what happened next didn't come as a complete surprise.

We were sitting on one of the double beds, when our eyes became dangerously deadlocked. In a matter of seconds, her warm lips were pressing against mine. Although brief, the kiss nearly exploded my heart. How could such a momentary act of affection so satisfy the soul and completely suck you dry at the same time? Sensory overload was setting in. I was about to lose control, but I couldn't. The journalist was going to be there in a couple of minutes.

When he arrived, the three of us decided on sushi for dinner. The yellow tail and fish eggs were quite good considering our distance from any ocean. I poured some sake into Aimee's cup and then mine. It was one of the few times I drank alcohol during the walk, but we were celebrating.

Sushi Supper and Sake Sippin': Aimee and the staff at a restaurant near Clarksville, Indiana.

Aimee and I hardly took our eyes off each other all night. Like powerful magnets, we were drawn together and difficult to pull apart. It hurt saying goodbye. She was crying, and I didn't know what to tell her. No, I just didn't have the courage to share my true feelings. I hated watching her drive away. The moment she was gone, I knew exactly what I wanted to say.

Aimee was all I could think about the next day. I wanted to know everything about her. Who was Aimee Elizabeth Reed? What did she like? Where did she come from? When would I see her again? Why did I let her go? How could we be together?

With Aimee on my mind, it was hard to pay proper attention to the dozens of people I met in southern Indiana. It was hard paying attention to anything until someone in a passing turquoise sedan lit a bunch of fireworks and threw them at me. I stood and watched the deafening barrage of crack and bang only a few steps away thinking, "Surely y'all have something better to do."

At six feet, four inches tall, I must have looked like a big yellow target. People would throw all kinds of things at me. Anything from trash, to food, to full soda cans. Rarely did they score a direct hit, but it certainly worked on my self-esteem. The early Fourth of July celebration had come only a couple miles from Scottsburg. I wasn't going to let it ruin my day. After all, I was doing a little celebrating of my own.

The lobby was enormous, decorated with expensive furniture and intricate wood paneling. When our eyes met, I knew it was real. She ran to me and slung her arms around my neck. I picked her up off the ground, embracing her warm body as close as possible.

A few dozen miles couldn't keep Aimee and I apart. She had driven up to Scottsburg so she could walk with me. Seymour was our destination, but as far as I was concerned, anywhere would do, as long as I was with her.

After dinner with one of my old college buddies, Aimee and I headed back to our hotel room.

"Tomorrow's going to be a long day," she said.

"Yeah, we better get some sleep."

It was the truth, but it wasn't what I really wanted. I could have listened to her soothing voice all night. Aimee had worked as a radio reporter before the American Cancer Society. She had a real knack for bringing a story to life.

We laid in the same bed that night with plenty of room between us. Despite my desire to hold her as we fell asleep, I wanted to treat Aimee with all the respect that she deserved. Some kind of tension was growing, and she broke the silence.

"What are you wearing?"

My sleep attire consisted of a sweater and my walking pants. Still, I played dumb.

"What?"

"Aren't you burning up?" she asked. I hadn't really noticed the beads of sweat on my forehead. I was roasting.

"And what's this?" She asked referring to the pouch I carried around my neck, which held my credit card and driver's license.

"That thing's gonna choke you in the night," she said laughing.

I couldn't help but laugh, too. She had a great sense of humor. I admired her. Even after everything she'd been through, Aimee still loved life.

Scottsburg to Seymour was no easy jaunt. Twenty-two miles was a long way to walk for someone who wasn't used to it. Aimee was in great shape, but fatigue and dehydration were taking a toll on her body.

We passed a bank sign that read 92 degrees. It was getting hotter, and I was worried that Aimee was taking too much sun. Looking for a place to stop for water, I noticed a big black flash out of the corner of my eye. In less than a second I spun around, ready to defend us.

"Don't worry, she ain't gonna hurt ya."

William Toppe was right. His dog Lucy was harmless. The black lab mix was wagging her tail so hard that it was moving her whole

Lucy's Love in Indiana.

body. Lucy eagerly sniffed our legs and the ground around us, much like any other dog, but she was far from ordinary.

Lucy was a cancer survivor, something she had in common with her owner. William had been diagnosed with colon cancer four years earlier, and Lucy was there to help him get through one of the most difficult times in his life. They had been there for each other.

"She's my best friend," William said.

After our visit to Kosair, I knew Aimee was compassionate for people, but she loved animals, too. Lucy loved her right back.

Lucy was ready to walk with us, and she would have if William hadn't held on to her collar. It reminded me of Shy, my first canine for cancer research.

William gave us some much-needed ice water, but it wasn't enough. Before long, we had to take another break. Aimee was dizzy, nauseous, and could hardly walk. I offered to carry her the rest of the way, but she insisted that she was ok.

Aimee and I in Indiana.

Finally we walked around a bend in the road, and I saw something. "Look!"

Aimee could barely hold her head up. "What?" she said weakened by the lack of fluids.

"Is that a store?" I asked.

It had one of those neon "OPEN" signs in the window. Without another word, Aimee took off. The building was only about a mile away. When we got there, the front door was open.

"Hello?" I said. No one answered. Whoever ran that place was definitely in the pyrotechnics business. There was nothing but fireworks. I wondered if that was where the pranksters outside of Scottsburg did their shopping.

Disappointed, Aimee and I walked back outside. Within a couple minutes, a man in his 40's staggered toward us from around a corner of the store, holding a can of beer.

"Sir, do you sell anything to drink here?" I asked hopefully.

"Just fireworks," he said with a heavy southern accent.

"How 'bout a water fountain?"

"Naw, just fireworks." He took a seat in a folding chair and cracked open the cold one. From the looks of it, it wasn't his first of the day.

"Hold on a sec." The man grunted and stretched for a cordless phone that was under his chair. Staring at the keypad as if it had just insulted him, he dialed a number and waited.

"Y'all pick up!" he blurted. "Yeah, hey, bring me a cupla ice waters," he paused briefly and continued in an agitated tone. "Cause there's a cupla people out here that's thirsty, that's why!"

Suddenly, the screen door on a trailer next to the store opened and two heads popped out.

"Let's go!" the man shouted. Shortly, a young girl and a little boy appeared with two glasses of ice water. The kids were amazed at how fast we were downing the frosty fluid.

"So what're y'all up to?" asked the man.

"We're walking across the country for cancer research," I said.

"Both of you?" he asked.

Aimee took a break from her water. "Well actually I'm just walking with him today to Seymour."

"Well aren't you a lazy ass?" he smirked.

"Are you kidding me?" I said glaring at him. "I'd like to see you out here walking."

"I gotta make money," he slurred, "I got kids and an actual job."

"This *is* my job," I said.

My job was to keeping walking, and every day I walked, I was that much further from Aimee. A few days later, she met me in

Indianapolis and walked with me to Brownsburg. It was raining for most of the day, but it didn't matter. We were together.

Clive, Aimee and I just outside of Brownsburg, Indiana.

CHAPTER 6

Land of Lincoln

efore the walk, I lifted weights and got on a treadmill three or four times a week. I wanted to be in "top walking shape," but I should've been trying to pack on the pounds. A dietician told me that I'd need to eat at least 6,000 calories a day just to keep up with my weight. She also gave me a list of things to eat and not to eat. I threw that list out after the first week of walking.

Keeping a healthy diet was important to me, but finding food was difficult at times. I had to eat anything and everything, including what I liked to call GSDs, or gas station delicacies—pickled pigs feet, potted meat, pork rinds, and those little neon pink hot dogs. I even ate some plants on the side of the road. Butterfly weed and yucca are surprisingly tasty but aren't very filling.

No matter how hungry I got, my favorite was coffee and pie. The simple combination tasted great and whisked away my worries when things weren't going well.

Coffee and pecan pie in Illinois.

❧

Some say the Midwest begins with Illinois. Others say Indiana, but one thing's for sure: There's no shortage of corn or soy out there. As it turns out, most of the corn and soy produced in the U.S. isn't grown for people to eat. I was told about 90 percent of it goes to feeding livestock.

Crossing a section of soy in the Great Midwest.

Heavy winds knocked me around as I made my way into Illinois. Just over the border, I stopped at a store. At first, David and Theresa Wright, the owners, thought I was a vagrant, but when I told them my story they invited me to stay at their house for the evening. That night, they introduced me to their friends Maurice and Charlotte Morse. Maurice and Charlotte were a lot like Pete and Sunshine when we met. We hugged and they treated me like family from the start.

Maurice and Charlotte had been married for nearly 26 years, and it was evident that they were still very much in love. In a society rife with divorce and broken families, they were the kind of couple that provided hope for long-term relationships. They'd be there for each other, no matter what.

Charlotte had been battling breast cancer for over a year. Through chemotherapy, radiation, and even major surgery she'd kept an upbeat attitude. For her, it was just another part of life.

"Ok, I've got cancer," she said, "This is me."

"It's brought us even closer together," Maurice said smiling at Charlotte. "If that's possible."

Charlotte and Maurice Morse.

There were a lot of compassionate people in the Illinois. In Ogden, I was just laying in my tent when a woman and two kids walked up to me.

"Hello, are you Eric?" the woman asked.

"Yeah." I thought it kind of odd that she already knew my name.

"I'm Kim Nigg," she said and then pointed to each of the kids. "This is my son Clayton and my niece, Kambry."

Kim lived in Ogden. Her mother Cindy Collins, who lived nearby in Urbana, read about me in the paper. Cindy lost her husband Dennis to cancer exactly five years before that day. She knew that I was supposed to be in Ogden, so she sent Kim to find me. I got to meet most of their family at Kim's house that night.

Stacy Orcutt, Collin Orcutt, Cindy Collins, Clayton Nigg, Kambry Orcutt, and Kim Nigg at her house in Ogden, Illinois.

They told me all about Dennis, his job as highway commissioner, his passion for woodworking, and how he got cancer. Doctors gave him six months to live. About two years after his diagnosis, Dennis was still going to work every morning until one day he was having trouble getting dressed. Cindy asked him to stay home that day. A few hours later he slipped into a coma. Two days later, Dennis passed away.

"The hardest part was watching him and not feeling like we could do anything," Cindy said.

Dennis was a lot of things to his family—a husband, a dad, a papa, a workingman, a joker, a storyteller, and a skilled woodworker. He was the glue that bonded the Collins family. Dennis may have been gone, but he certainly wasn't lost. Cindy and each of her daughters had pieces of furniture that he built by hand in their homes. And, they were always on the lookout for papa pennies. When they'd find pennies—in pajamas, on vacation in Mexico, and other strange spots—they believed that Dennis was with them.

From that day on, I picked up papa pennies. They seemed to be everywhere. Finding them always made me think about Cindy and her family. It made me think about Dennis. Sometimes I'd just look up and smile when I'd find one. Other times, I'd say something to him as if he were there. I hoped Dennis was watching over me, too.

My first papa penny in Illinois.

We all had tears in our eyes after talking about Dennis, but it must've been funny watching Cindy and I hug. She was more than a foot shorter than me.

"It was so great to meet you," I said.

"You never know when you're going to see us again," she said.

In such a short time, that family started to feel like my own. I didn't want to leave them. I felt like stopping and settling down, but Cindy and her family were the exact reason why I was walking. Kambry, Kim, and Clayton walked me to the edge of town the next morning.

A few miles out of Ogden, a car pulled up beside me. It was Maurice and Charlotte Morse. Charlotte said she was going to walk with me. At first, I didn't think it was such a great idea. Charlotte was battling stage-four breast cancer, undergoing treatment, and she was going to walk with me under the hot sun. Not only did Charlotte walk with me, she walked eight miles!

Kambry, Kim, and Clayton

Cindy Collins and Charlotte Morse near Urbana, Illinois.

All day, Maurice followed us in the car. He brought us lunch, water, and a lot of encouragement. He even got out and walked for a couple of miles while Charlotte drove the car. Maurice was quite the jovial soul. He always had a smile on his face, a great attitude about life, and he waved at all the cars passing by.

When we made it to the outskirts of Urbana, we were greeted by Cindy Collins. We met her daughter Stacy and walked to Carle Hospital.

While I was getting a tour of Carle Cancer Center, I got a call on my cell phone. My heart dropped. It was Aimee. She'd driven there to see me. Quickly, I walked outside and made my way to the main road. I started looking in all directions. Then there she was, wearing a pink shirt, standing on the other side of street. It felt like electricity was running through my body causing my fingertips and toes to tingle. Like lost soul mates reunited, we hugged like we'd never lose each other again. On that busy street corner, nothing else mattered—Aimee and I were together again.

She'd set up lodging for us at a hotel on the other side of town, which meant I still had a few miles to walk. She drove by me a couple of times and stopped so we could hug and kiss. We needed each other, and nothing was going to keep us apart.

The next day, Aimee walked with me to Mansfield. A local journalist walked with us for a while, but he was picked up after a couple of miles.

Aimee, Erik Potter and I outside of Champaign, Illinois.

Once Aimee and I were alone, we talked about everything, about her work, about Louisville, the places I'd been, and the people I'd met. We met quite a few people that day. Maybe that's why we didn't get a chance to talk about us and how we felt about each other.

Kim and Clayton walked with us for the last few miles into Mansfield. When we got there, they took us back to our hotel room. Instead of eating out, Aimee and I went to the store and bought a bunch of finger foods. We laid in our bed that night and fed each other "bites" of bread, hummus, olives, pepperonis, and cheese. I loved that about her. She enjoyed the little things in life.

She drove me back to Mansfield the next day. Little red splotches formed on her neck and face as she cried. I wished that we could've gotten lost like we did on the first day we met. It was tearing me apart, but that's how it went. We'd meet, walk, and ride an emotional roller coaster. Then she'd drive back to Louisville, and I'd walk further away, not knowing when, or if, we'd see each other again.

We hugged and I got out of her Escape. She started driving away slowly. It felt like my guts were being torn out. She stopped a couple of times, prolonging the inevitable, looking into her rearview mirror. I wanted to run after her, pull her door open, hug her and kiss her, tell her not to leave, tell her that I wanted to spend the rest of my life with her, but I couldn't and I didn't.

Finally, I just started walking, looking over my shoulder. The first two times, she was still waiting in her Escape, but the third time she was gone. Later that day, I found another letter from her. It read:

06/19/2005

Eric (WAA Founder & Managing Member)

As I sit here and & watch you work, my heart aches because I know it's only a matter of a very short time before we'll have to say, "I'll see you soon" again. I truly do not want to leave you. By the way, I love your look right now—no shirt, lucky Pirates hat—you are so adorable, even when you're not trying to be. When I look at you, sometimes I still can't believe this is happening. Where'd you come from, Eric Latham? It's almost like you're an angel. You're so pure and compassionate. I've never met another person like you. When we're together, I'm completely at ease. When we're together, the whole world stands still. All of my worries & fears just disappear. Looking into your eyes takes me to a place I've never been & a place I don't ever want to leave. It's so amazing how even when we're together, I still miss you. I know we've talked about that before, but it's so true. Every part of me longs to be near you. I can't wait until I'm back in your arms again in three weeks. Every day until then, I'll be thinking of the moment when our eyes meet & we get those HUGE smiles across our faces. I just caught you looking at me! BUSTED!! Eric, you are so incredible. You totally amaze me. Thank you for making me the happiest girl on the planet. My life will never be the same since you've "walked" into it.

Love, Aimee
(an extremely helpful ACS representative)
"Ya'll pick up!"

CHAPTER 7

The Hawkeye State

While planning Walk About America 2005, I researched people who tried to walk across the United States. I found that many of them didn't complete their journey, primarily because of poor planning. Either they ran out of money, had nothing to eat, no place to stay, or experienced health problems. Some, who simply became bored, weren't taking steps with a purpose. Only a few endured initiation into the cross-country club, and there was a reason for that. Literally walking across the U.S. is not an easy task, but from day one I knew that failure in completing my own journey to San Francisco was not an option.

Many people spoke of other cross-country walkers. I always hoped to find them, someone who truly understood what my mind and body were going through. As it turned out, the only person I met along the way who had completed a walk across the country found *me* first.

〜

Two men in dress shirts, tucked neatly into their suit pants, approached me as I was walking through Davenport, Iowa. Their ties bounced around in the wind, anchored only by their starch-steady collars. They walked side by side until one took the lead, smiled, and spoke with an English accent.

"You're the guy walking across the country, aren't you?" He asked.

In one form or another, I'd probably been asked that question a thousand times already, but I liked hearing it. Not for personal recognition but because it made me feel like the campaign was making an impact.

John Freeman understood that feeling. He was a veteran member of the cross-country club. In 1985, John had walked from New York City to Mexico for Hospice and Children's Terminal Care.

As we stood on the side of the road, in our own little world, sharing stories and commiserating about similar experiences, it was amazing, even 20 years after his walk, how much he remembered.

I imagined the instant bond formed between John and I was similar to the one between Joe Vanderpool, his mother-in-law, and all the people I met affected by cancer. There's comfort in finding someone who's been through, or is going through, the same thing you are.

Marty Ellison and John Freeman in Davenport, Iowa.

Quenching my thirst was nearly impossible during the walk, but by the time I reached Iowa, I'd become a pro at chugging cold beverages. Like a maniac, I'd empty the contents of a can in a matter of seconds and come up gasping for air. The woman behind the counter was only slightly impressed.

I was about to throw away the can when she said, "You know, we'll give you a nickel for that."

"Really?"

"You can redeem any pop can for a nickel in Iowa," she said opening the cash register and digging out a shiny new nickel. A lightbulb went off in my head as I handed over the can.

It was a simple operation. There were all kinds of cans along the side of the road, so I began picking them up and stuffing them into plastic grocery bags. One bag could hold 23 or 24 cans before they started falling out. When I turned them in, I'd donate the money to the American Cancer Society. It wasn't much, but I figured every little bit helped. Plus, I was cleaning up the highway. I thought of calling this sub-campaign, "Cans for a Cure," but the title might have been severely misconstrued.

Picking up "Cans for a Cure" between Davenport and Plain View, Iowa.

After meeting little Abbie in Charleston, West Virginia, I wanted to visit more cancer treatment facilities and hospitals along the way. That's where I'd meet real people battling cancer, who inspired me to keep going.

Isabelle Thomas was staring out the window when I walked into her room at St. Luke's Hospital in Cedar Rapids. The sun was shining, but she was on the verge of discontent.

The 82-year-old woman had been in and out of the hospital for a quarter of a century, battling four different types of cancer: breast cancer (since 1980), skin cancer, chronic Leukemia (since 1990), and Lymphoma. Still, Isabelle's love for life was obvious and her sense of humor was wonderful. It was July 4th, and all she wanted was her independence from the hospital.

"What're you doing tonight?" I asked.

"My doctor says I should have a good view of the fireworks from here," she said.

"I've got nothing to do," I said, "Would you mind if I came back up here and watched them with you?"

"Sure," she said.

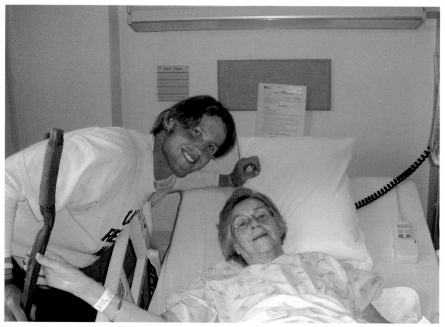

Isabelle Thomas at St. Luke's Hospital in Cedar Rapids, Iowa.

Isabelle was surprised when I got back to the hospital that night. She said she wasn't sure if I was going to show up, but I wouldn't have missed it for the world. Neither of us wanted to be alone on the Fourth of July.

I brought award-winning caramels and she arranged for the nurse to bring us orange sherbet. The doctor wasn't lying about the fireworks. I'm sure we had one of the best views in the hospital. While Isabelle and I sat in the dark, mesmerized by the rainbow colored bursts, I wondered what Aimee was doing.

When it was over, the nurse flipped on the lights. Isabelle and I smiled at each other. Before leaving, I gave her a hug. When I pulled away, she still held my hand while tears formed in her eyes.

"I'll never forget our Fourth of July party," she said.

"Me neither," I said fighting off a lump in the back of my throat.

Fireworks show through Isabelle's Hospital Room.

I squeezed her hand once more and headed for the door. I hated leaving Isabelle, but that's how it worked. I'd walk into people's lives, tell them things were going to be ok, tell them they weren't alone, and then I'd leave them. I felt like I was letting so many people down.

Fourth of July Celebration with Isabelle.

Cedar Rapids was the last real city I'd see for a while. Most towns across Iowa were about eight to ten miles apart. I was told that was how far people could get in their covered wagons when they were moving west many years ago. It was a tough life, and I felt their pain.

My goal was to walk 17-25 miles a day. Many times it was more than that, especially as I moved further west. Sometimes I was lucky just to find food and fresh water. Finding a safe place to camp was not always easy either.

When I arrived in Colo, there were barely any cars or people around. I walked through the streets looking for the center square. While I was at the Post Office, sending donations to the American Cancer Society, I ran into the fire chief and told him about my situation.

"Well, you can camp behind the fire station," he said. "There's just one catch."

"What's that?"

"It's the first night of the festival, and that's where it kicks off," he said.

I set up my tent about 20 feet from the fire station, and within two hours, it was swarming with people. The fire chief invited me to take part in the festivities, so I got some food and headed up to the first big event of the night.

Main Street was packed for the outhouse races. Two teams competed at a time. Each team consisted of four people. One brave soul would get inside the outhouse while the other three pushed them down the road. The person inside the outhouse had to stop and perform all kinds of tasks before racing toward the finish line.

Outhouse Races at the Crossroads Festival in Colo, Iowa.

After the outhouse races, everybody gathered around a huge mud pit lit up by floodlights. It was Pig Mania 2005. People were getting into the mud and chasing pigs. The object of Pig Mania was to catch a pig and lift it up over a fence onto a mattress. I was speaking with a local journalist about the campaign three rows back, but I still got mud all over me.

Pig Mania at the Crossroads Festival in Colo, Iowa.

The journalist and I were taking some pictures when someone from the crowd said, "Y'all should do it."

The woman on the loudspeaker agreed. She yelled to all the people who were starting to leave. "Wait, wait, wait, y'all! We've got one more match up for you!"

I had only one pair of clothes, but I knew I'd never get the chance to wrestle pigs again. The journalist and I climbed into the cold, slimy mud. Two pigs were released, and we chased them all over the ring. Somehow I got mine first and put it over the fence onto the mattress.

"Winner!" The woman said over the loud speaker. The crowd cheered.

Walker Gone Wild: Joining in on the pig wrestling festivities.

Twenty-four days had passed since I met Cindy Collins and her family. I thought about them as I walked into Ogden, Iowa. That's where I reached 1,500 miles, which was probably worth celebrating, but every part of my body ached. Each time I exhaled, a great sum of pain entrenched deep in my bones, peaked. It was the kind of pain that could literally brings a man to his knees, in a ditch, on the side of a road. Walking every day took a lot of self-discipline, but people like Cindy and her family kept me going.

Nobody was going to help me cross the Missouri River. The bridge was not for walkers. It was like walking over a huge cheese grater with rusty holes almost big enough to put your foot through.

Crossing the Missouri River into Nebraska.

CHAPTER 8

The Cornhusker State

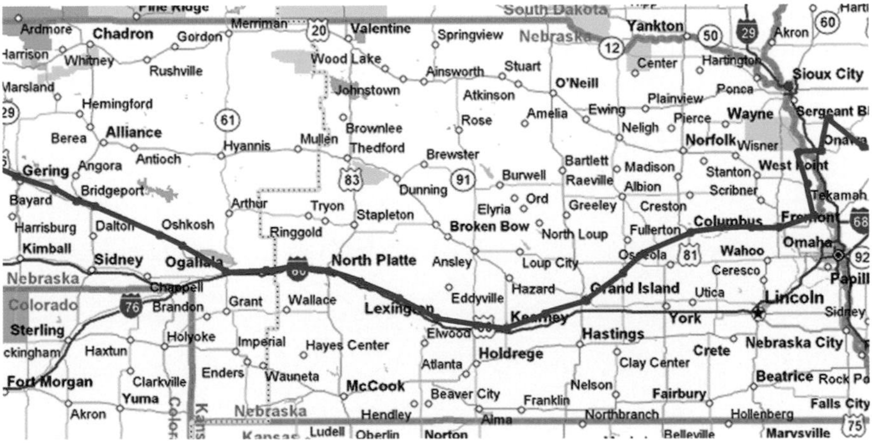

It was a perfect match. They were tan, full-figured, youthful, and smelled wonderful—at least in the beginning. Yes, these were good boots. They had to be. After all, the well being of my feet depended on their quality. I had arranged to pick up my second pair of Montrail boots in Nebraska.

The airport in North Platte wasn't very big, but for some reason, the parking lot was packed. As I approached the terminal, a woman scurried up to me.

"Eric—Are you Eric?" Out of breath, she handed me a pair of boots, "Here you go."

The second I got a closer look I knew something was wrong.

"Um, these aren't the my boots." The boots she brought looked as if they had barely survived World War II, not to mention they were about five sizes too small. I felt bad after seeing the look on her face. She was genuinely disappointed. Trying to clear up the confusion, I lifted up one of my feet.

"They should look like this."

The woman thought about it for a few seconds. Suddenly, it hit her like a ton of bricks.

"I think I picked up the wrong box," she said wanting badly to fix the situation. "Wait here. I'll be right back."

She returned in an hour with the right boots. I was relieved. My feet hurt just thinking of wearing the first pair any longer. They'd lasted 1,962 miles.

❧

The shortest day I ever walked was from Onawa, Iowa to Decatur, Nebraska. It was only eight miles, but after crossing the bridge of death, I needed a break. The Green Lantern looked like a good place to cool off.

There were a few middle-aged men drinking beer at the bar. I pulled up a stool. A woman behind the bar asked, "What can I get ya, hun?"

"Just a water on the rocks," I said. The man sitting next to me turned in his stool.

"What's the pack for?" he asked.

"I'm walking across the country."

"Why in the hell would ya do that?" He laughed with support from his chuckle orchestra. Most of those guys were already drunk, and it was only 2 p.m.

"To raise money for cancer research." It didn't quite have the sobering effect I was hoping for, but they did ask a lot of questions.

The man sitting next to me introduced himself as Toolie. He asked me to join him and his buddies at a table. They drank beer after beer, remembering old times. Within an hour, I knew most of their stories, where they were from, how they got there, and what they did for a living. Toolie was starting to get sloppy. Suddenly, he slammed a wad of crumbled cash on the table as if he was angry.

"As our guest of honor," he said slurring, "I want to buy ya dinner."

Toolie grinned and pointed to a sign behind the bar.

"You're having the special tonight." The neon sign said:

"Special Wednesday: Turkey Fries."

Toolie couldn't wait for my response. "You ever have Turkey Fries before?"

"No, but they sound good," I said. I figured they were like chicken tenders, but from the look on Toolie's face, something was up. He and his buddies were having a good laugh, possibly the best they'd had all night. Toolie yelled to the waitress and tried to keep a straight face.

"We'll take one order of turkey fries for the gentleman," he said pointing to me.

She looked at me with a smile. "You sure you want that?"

Looking around the table, something was definitely up, but you can't beat a free meal. "Sure, sounds good."

The table erupted in laughter one more time. When I walked up to the bar to get an iced tea, the bartender smiled at me and shook her head.

"You know they're turkey balls right?" She asked.

"Huh?"

"Nuts. Testicles." She hesitated. "The Turkey fries."

Turkey Fries at The Green Lantern in Decatur, Nebraska.

I looked back at my table. They were all waiting for me to turn around before they started laughing. One guy was literally slapping his knee and another was laughing so hard he started choking and coughing.

At first, the idea of eating turkey testicles wasn't very appetizing. They brought me a full plate with fries and tartar dipping sauce. For some reason they were chewy, but I ate every one of them, and they weren't that bad.

Turkey Fries at The Green Lantern in Decatur, Nebraska.

Nebraska was longest state I had to cross. Along the way, I made many friends, but there was one person who was always on my mind. Aimee and I had talked about flying her into Omaha so we could meet somewhere. When I got to Blair, I tried to call her, but she never picked up. We were losing touch, and it was killing me. She had her own life, and I had to keep walking. Lonely, I made my way across Nebraska.

Not too many people had ever heard of Havens. One woman told me that it was just an old abandoned dance hall on the side of the road. Getting there wasn't as easy as I hoped. I was just walking along when someone in a truck launched a taco at me as they drove by.

"Wish you luck!" They said (or something very similar to that).

I wasn't mad because they threw a taco at me but because I was starving. I stared it in the gravel for at least five minutes. They'd sacrificed a perfectly good soft taco supreme to commit a "walker hate crime." Who throws a soft taco, anyway? They were obviously novice taco-tossers.

There really was an old abandoned dance hall in Havens. It was in ruins. Still, I had to find a place to camp, so I sat in the gravel driveway hoping to meet someone. After about an hour, a truck pulled up. There was a man behind the wheel and a woman riding

'Taco Tosser' commits walker hate crime between Columbus and Havens, Nebraska.

in the passenger seat. I told them about the walk and asked if they knew of a safe place to camp.

"Our trailer is just up that'ah way, the man said sizing me up, "You can camp in our yard."

His name was John Staniec, and his wife Rosemary was sitting next to him. I got to meet the whole Staniec family that night, including their daughter Kim, who had survived cervical cancer.

The Staniec's in Havens, Nebraska.

During dinner, I looked out a window and noticed a horse. Turning to John, I asked, "Is that your horse?"

"Yep," he said, "Like to ride her?"

"Are you serious?" I'd never ridden a horse before, but it was another opportunity I couldn't pass up.

Riding Jasmine in Havens, Nebraska.

From the moment I got on her, Jasmine knew that I was a first-timer. She wouldn't move. I tried everything—whistling, clapping, snapping, and even singing, but she wasn't about to budge. Finally, when the Staniecs gave me a cowboy hat and frayed leather jacket, Jasmine began trotting around the yard. John branded me with a new nickname: Hot to Trot.

"You ever fire a gun?" John asked.

"Well, once…no not really," I said.

"Want to?"

"Sure, why not?"

They set up some plastic milk jugs filled with water, and John handed me a six-shooter. My hand was shaking as I fired off a couple of rounds. Of course, I didn't come close to hitting anything.

"Boy, you couldn't hit the broad side of a barn," John said laughing. He was enjoying it all a little too much.

"That was pretty fun," I said.

"If you liked that, you gotta try this other one," John said.

First time firing a gun in Havens, Nebraska.

John ran off and returned with a pretty hefty rifle.

"It's Russian," he said as he handed me the gun. "Now hold her steady."

I held it up to my shoulder and fired off a round. A three-foot flame burst from the barrel.

"Damn," I said examining the smoking rifle. The butt of the gun hit my shoulder like a stern punch. It was going to leave a bruise.

"Yep, I know," John said, "This beauty was made during the cold war."

I couldn't help but wonder if a piece of steel like that was legal.

Most of Nebraska was rural, which meant I couldn't use my cell phone or computer, but I did I received an email from a guy named Tyler Weig. Earlier in the summer, Tyler had ridden his bicycle across the country to also raise money for the American Cancer Society. In fact, we just missed each other in Iowa, his home state. While I was walking through Ames going west, he was only 35 miles south of me in Des Moines going east.

After he finished, Tyler said he'd seen my web site and wanted to come out and walk with me for a couple of weeks, so we decided to meet in Scottsbluff. On the first morning, we headed for Henry, my last stop in the Cornhusker state.

Tyler Weig of Cycling for a Cure 2005 in Scottsbluff, Nebraska.

Tyler and I were friends from the start. We had a lot in common, strongly believing in community service and more specifically joining the fight against cancer. He understood some of the mental and physical challenges I was facing.

Physically, my body was taking a real beating. I was constantly bandaging my feet. Sharp pains shot up and down my back, caused by the 60-pound pack I was carrying. My weak knees trembled, and I was losing weight every week. But in spite of all the physical maladies, I'd say it was more difficult mentally.

Every day, I was meeting people who'd share their cancer stories with me. Some days I'd laugh with them. Some days I'd cry. And I had plenty of time to think about them. Hundreds of faces were flashing through my head, day and night. Unfortunately, some of those people lost their battles with cancer while I was still walking. I'd receive a phone call or an email from a family member or friend.

People I loved were dying, and I couldn't do a thing about it. That hurt worse than any blister, back pain, or sore knees. I would've given my life for Austin Staples, little Abbie, Isabelle Thomas, or any of the hundreds of other people I met who had cancer. Their amazing energy, courage, and strength to keep going inspired me. That's why I was walking. That's why Tyler was walking.

We learned early that Tyler the biker was not the same as Weig the walker. He was in good physical shape, but bicycling and walking are just two different types of exercising. Plus, he'd been off his bike for over a month by then.

Tyler was falling behind. He was getting blisters and dehydration was setting in. We stopped a few times to get cold drinks, but that wasn't helping. We were a few miles outside of Henry when the man who we were going to stay with there, pulled up in his truck.

"I know ya can't take ride," he said, "but what if I took your bags into town?"

"Thanks." Tyler didn't waste any time, tossing his pack in the truck. They looked at me.

"I'll keep mine," I said. I'd carried my pack the entire way and wasn't about to stop.

Ditching his pack helped Tyler finish the walk into Henry, but he was having second thoughts about the whole thing. He wasn't sure if he could go on.

CHAPTER 9

The Equality State

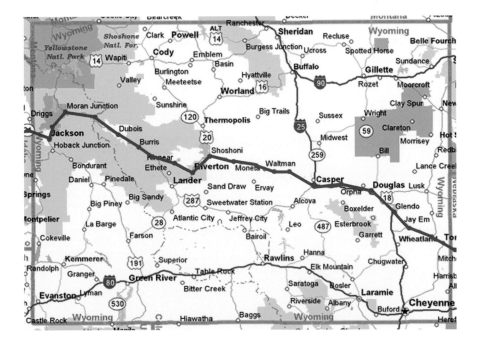

From the start, one of the most difficult things was trying to convince people that I was going to walk across the country. By the end, it was even more difficult convincing them that I had already done it. There were some people who never believed me.

"You're doing what?" the man asked, one arm hanging out of his truck window.

We were in central Wyoming, where snakes outnumber people and sweet sage covers everything but the highway.

"Believe or not I used to stick out my thumb," he said looking off into the distance, reliving some of his more adventurous days. "Well, you know how hitchhiking goes."

"No really—I'm literally walking," I was getting irritated. For some reason it bothered me. I had walked thousands of miles, and this guy wasn't going to take that away from me. Then he put me over the edge.

"C'mon—I'll take ya into Riverton," he said waving me over. It was hopeless.

"Thank you, but I can't." I just started walking again. It was my 199th ROP. Not accepting ROPs, or rides offered for progress, was one of my rules. It would've defeated my purpose.

Sage and snakes in central Wyoming.

❧

Tyler thought about it over night, but he was through walking. It didn't mean was he going back to Iowa, though. He'd driven to Nebraska in his green Ford Taurus, or the "tortoise" as he called it, and decided he would provide a support vehicle for about a week.

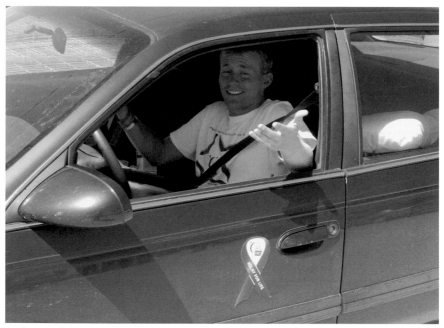

Tyler and the Tortoise in Wyoming.

Tyler brought water, food, and much needed support during some very lonely times. He'd write encouraging messages in chalk along the highway, and check out the terrain so there'd be no surprises. After learning about papa pennies, he'd leave "nanny nickels" for me to find. He was also very good at driving ahead to meet our contacts, set up dinner, or meetings.

Tyler knew what it meant to have a support vehicle. He had one during his bike across the country, but walking is a different story. It's a lot slower, and I could tell Tyler was getting bored. He spent a lot of time waiting on me, passing time by reading or throwing rocks at old road signs. When I'd catch up to him, we'd talk for a while, and I'd start walking again.

Tyler wasn't completely done walking. Sometimes he'd drive ahead, leave his car, and meet up with me. We were both sore at the end of each day.

Call a chiropractor: Outside of Glenrock, Wyoming.

The best thing about Tyler was his enthusiasm. When I reached my scheduled stops, he'd clap and cheer. He'd even scream the town's name, and I'd always join him.

At the end of each day, we'd talk about the ups and downs of our journeys, the towns we'd been through, and the people we'd met. We also talked about our campaigns and how sometimes people misunderstood our goals. It wasn't just about giving money. It was about joining the fight against cancer and making a difference in our communities. Tyler and I had become good friends, and I hated to see him leave. When we reached Casper, he drove back to Iowa.

After visiting Rocky Mountain Oncology, I stopped at the ACS office in Casper. My relationship with ACS wasn't always a bed of roses. The local community relations manager hit me with a piece of news that nearly ended it all.

"Someone from headquarters called about you, but they said, 'Don't help Eric, he's doing this on his own.'"

My face was getting red, and I was ready to punch the wall. There were some ACS offices that wanted to help and some that didn't, but hearing that was just too much.

The woman apologized and tried to smooth things over by saying ACS never helped in my kind of events. Maybe she didn't know it, but that wasn't true. They'd given Tyler money for food, lodging, and supplies.

I thought about canceling the rest of the walk and cutting off any more donations to ACS. Then I thought I'd still raise money but donate it to another organization. After thinking about it all night, I decided to stay the course. There were a lot of good people who worked for ACS, and I was walking for people, not some organization. Plus, nothing was going to ruin my birthday.

On the day I turned 24 years old, I started walking to Natrona, which was about 26 miles from Casper. I walked all day. The sun was setting and I still hadn't gotten there, so I started looking for a safe place to camp. I saw a sign that said, "Brewer Ranch."

I knocked on the door and a woman, who appeared to be in her 40's, came out. Her blond hair was tied up in a ponytail. She wore tight wrangler jeans capped off with a belt buckle the size of a dinner plate.

"Yeah?"

"Are you Mrs. Brewer?" I asked.

"Yeah," she said. After I told her about the walk, she looked over at another house on the property.

"I've gotta ask my dad." She walked into the other house, and a minute later, an older man with a handlebar moustache and cowboy hat peered through the screen door. Then she came back outside.

"That'll be fine," she said.

"Thanks so much."

"There's just one thing," she said, "You're gonna want to camp in the corral, and make sure you lock the gate."

"Why's that?"

"We've got free range horses that can get pretty curious," she said.

I made my way up to the corral and wrapped a heavy chain around the gate.

Birthday sunset at the Brewer Ranch near Natrona, Wyoming.

After watching a gorgeous sunset, I set up my tent and crawled in. I celebrated my birthday with a protein bar and water. I had some crackers, but I decided to save those for an emergency.

As I stared at the crystal clear constellations in the sky, I thought about all the gifts I'd been given that year—a loving family, supportive friends, and the opportunity to meet thousands of people because of the walk. I'd never forget the year I turned 24.

I woke up that night to a strange sound.

"Clang...clang."

It was still dark, so I grabbed my flashlight.

"Clang...clang, clang."

Slowly, I unzipped my tent and looked outside.

"Clang." It was coming from the corral gate.

"Clang....Clang....Clang." I couldn't believe what I saw when I lifted up my flashlight. A stallion was slamming into the corral gate. I stayed awake for a few minutes, wondering if the chain was going to hold, but fatigue defeated concern and the curtain fell on my birthday.

I'd never been to Wyoming before, but from the maps and what people had told me, I knew the stretch from Casper to Riverton was going to biggest challenge yet. If I was going to get enough food or water to survive, I'd have to be smart about it—or really lucky.

On my way to Hiland, I saw a green Ford Taurus on the side of the road.

"Tyler!" I yelled running up to the car. The person who got out wasn't Tyler. It was an ACS volunteer from Casper, but it made me realize how important Tyler's support had been, and out in the middle of Wyoming, I needed his help more than ever.

That wasn't the first time I'd be fooled by a Ford. Every time I saw a white Ford Escape, I thought Aimee had come back. It made me think about the first time I met her, the first time we held hands, the first time we kissed. And every time a white Ford Escape would drive by without stopping, I'd think about the time she left me in Mansfield.

When I arrived in Hiland, the wind was blowing in all directions. Through the dust and tumbleweed hopping across the highway, I saw a sign. It said:

Hiland, Wyoming
Population   10

Hiland was home to Steelman's Brightspot. When I walked through the front door, an older woman was sitting at the counter reading a newspaper.

"So there's ten people in Hiland, huh?" I asked.

"There ain't that many," she said without looking up from the paper, "But we got one more now that you're here." She smirked at me.

Small towns out west usually had one place to get supplies, eat a meal, and get drunk. The Brightspot was one of those places. There were a few guys sitting at the bar when I walked in. They were real cowboys, wearing hats, boots, dust-covered coats, and leather faces. Many of them talked about their experiences with cancer. I wanted to take some pictures, but when I took out my camera one of the guys pulled back in his stool.

"Woah, woah, woah."

"What?" I pulled my camera out of the gym sock that I kept it in.

The cowboy relaxed and let out a sigh.

"Some of us keep our guns in socks like that," he said.

I was in bad shape when I walked into Riverton. The heat had gotten to me and severe dehydration was setting in. Fortunately Rocky Mountain Oncology had a branch there, and the nurse was very kind. She hooked me up to an IV so I could replenish my fluids. Soaking my bruised and blistered feet, I began to really wonder how I was going to make it another day, much less to San Francisco. At 163 pounds, I was literally withering away.

It looked like the end. I'd been without water for more than a day, and I couldn't walk any further. I tried to flag down the few cars, but nobody would stop.

Just then, a green Taurus blew by. It looked just like Tyler's, but so did the last one. I wasn't about to get my hopes up again. Suddenly the green Taurus came back around. It was Tyler and the Tortoise!

Cindy Collins and her family paid for him to come back out and help me. We were both amazed at their generosity. They didn't even know Tyler, and they gave him the money, no questions asked. Cindy was more than just a friend. She was family.

Tyler helped me start Wyoming, and he'd help me finish it off. For another week he brought me food, water, and good cheer. It was the only reason I made it over the continental divide, through Togwotee Pass, and into Jackson Hole, home of the Grand Tetons.

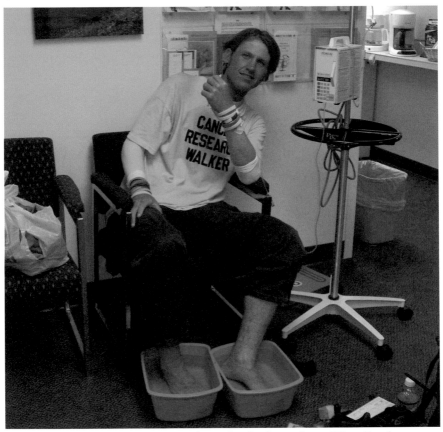

Battling Severe Dehydration: Taking fluids through an IV at Rocky Mountain Oncology in Riverton, Wyoming.

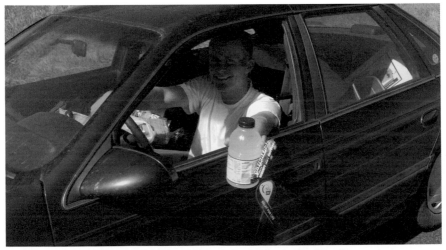

Back Again! Tyler and the Tortoise near Dubois, Wyoming.

Grand Teton near Jackson Hole, Wyoming.

When we reached Jackson, Tyler headed back to Iowa. Once again, I was all alone to face one of my greatest challenges—climbing Teton Pass. At nearly 85-hundred feet above sea level the wind was icy cold, and the ten percent grade was shredding my feet. It was a test, and I was the only one who could pass it.

Climbing Teton Pass near Jackson, Wyoming.

CHAPTER 10

The Gem State

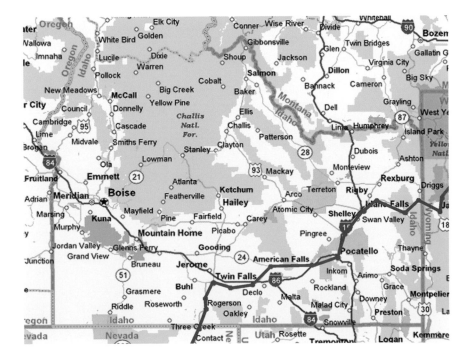

It was harvest time, and I was walking through the heart of potato country. Bingham County alone produces more spuds than the whole state of Maine. Idaho produces around 13.8 billion pounds a year.

Every potato starts as a piece of another potato. Ideally, it would be planted in the richest soil in the perfect climate. It would receive plenty of water, breathe the cleanest air, and be free from pests or disease, creating a large and healthy potato. Unfortunately, some spuds aren't given all or any of these conditions, depriving them the best chance to fully develop. They are a product of their environment. Some farmers will tell you that no matter how much you water potatoes, how much clean air they get, or how much you care for them, they'd never reach their full potential.

Massive machines with metal fingers moved from row to row, sifting through the earth. Like large hands, they sorted the potatoes, only keeping the biggest and best, while leaving behind those that were too small or misshapen. They'd waited their whole lives for harvest only to find out they weren't good enough.

Many of the discarded laid helpless next to the road, defined as useless because of their defects. I picked one up and dusted it off. It was small, oblong, and slightly green, but among billions of potatoes, it was unique. Most importantly, it was still a potato and always will be.

❧

The inevitability of spontaneous occurrence was very exciting. I'd get up each day, not knowing exactly what was going to happen or whom I was going to meet, but things were different when I reached Idaho. I spent most of my time there reflecting on the places I'd been, the people I'd met, and the person I was becoming.

The British Isles, France, Belgium, and an airport in Beijing—I'd done my fair share of traveling, but I'd never really seen my own country. It was something I always wanted to do, but I never imagined walking across it. I'm glad that I did.

Each of the nine states I'd been through were beautiful in their own way, and by walking, I developed a completely different perspective. I'd never experienced Rocky Mountain air, so fresh that it feels like the first time you ever took a breath; Midwest soil, so rich that it actually produces new ideas in your head, and sunshine out west, so warm that it melts away all your grudges and regrets.

I never really appreciated wild animals in their natural habitats, crystal clean streams, and fresh wildflowers. By walking, I saw every blade of grass and felt every stone beneath my boots. America is vast and geographically diverse, but people are our greatest strength.

Meeting thousands of people allowed me to learn a lot about Americans in general. Despite what people may say around the world, we're strong and compassionate. I saw countless communities rally to save their friends and family who were devastated by cancer.

Individuals and organizations built our country by making selfless contributions to their communities. As citizens of this great nation, we'll continue to bolster democracy through this time-honored tradition. Over the years, our precious democracy has been under attack. Those in power have made decisions based on their own agendas, and the majority has suffered because of it.

Sometimes I wish our elected officials would take the time to walk across their states. First east to west. Then north to south. Then diagonally. Then they should try it blind. Then deaf. Then gay. Then as a Muslim. Then as a soldier. Then in a wheelchair. Then without any money. Understanding people is the key to serving them.

Often I was asked, "Why'd you choose to walk? Why not bike or drive? You could still raise money for cancer research."

It was the best way to meet people. If I hadn't walked, a nurse and her caring husband might not have opened their home to a stranger, and still embraced me like a son. I might not have held a 17-month-old baby who was fighting for her life. I might not have fallen in love with the woman who changed me forever. I might not have shared award-winning caramels while watching fireworks with the sweetest 82-year-old woman I've ever met. If I hadn't walked, I wouldn't have gotten anywhere.

Nobody really walks anywhere anymore. Even just a hundred years ago, it was one of the primary forms of transportation. We've all heard about grandpa walking 14 miles to school, barefoot in the snow, uphill both ways. Things are a little different these days.

We shuffle around our homes and offices, then get into our cars and drive a few blocks to a convenience store, just to save a little time. Like handwriting a letter, walking has been replaced with technology, creating an impersonal society. More and more, we use cell phones and computers to communicate. Future generations will know no different.

The Internet provides us with infinite opportunities, but the free-flow of information has left us wondering whom to trust. Meaning is lost, and we're not sure what to believe. We've entered the Age of Paranoia and Skepticism.

It was hard enough walking thousands of miles, but being blatantly profiled made things a lot harder. I never knew exactly what people were thinking when they saw me. Those who knew nothing about me, probably thought I was homeless or down on my luck, but once they'd heard about my cause, I was suddenly some great philanthropist. Not everybody had to have a reason to help a stranger in need. Pete and Sunshine taught me that lesson early on.

We're all prejudice, whether we like it or not. Just by looking at someone, based on our previous experiences or what we've been told, we assume things about them. Assumption is a risky business. Even before meeting people, I was judged because of my clothing, hair, height, gender, and race. A man I'd never met drove up to me and asked if I wanted to smoke some pot with him.

"Why would you ask me that?" I said, wondering if he'd even read my shirt.

"Just thought you might be into that kinda stuff," he said.

Some people thought I was just a hippie-vagrant. Others thought I was dangerous and kept a close eye on me. There were even people who thought I was some kind of scam artist, stealing people's money in the name of cancer research. I took it personally at first, but then I realized it wasn't me causing all of the paranoia and skepticism, it's just the society that we've created.

By the time I'd reached Fort Hall, I was numb to it all. Ginger's Café wasn't very big. It could probably seat 20 people, but it was empty when I walked in. Dropping my pack on the floor, I sat on a stool at the counter. The waitress, who seemed surprised to have a customer, handed me a menu. By the look on her face, she was wondering how I was going to pay for my meal.

"The special's vegetable-beef soup," she said.

"I'll take it." Even though it felt like a hundred degrees outside, I found that going with the flow in these kinds of situations made things a lot easier. I could've just told her that I was walking across the country for cancer research. People usually warmed right up to me then, but I didn't like that. It made me feel like I had to validate my reason for being. I wanted to be treated like everyone else.

I was finishing up my soup when a couple of guys walked in. They sat at a table behind me and ordered some food. One of our basic human needs is to communicate with others. I could've just finished my lunch, paid, and hit the road, but I craved conversation. And, if there was an opportunity to learn something, I took it.

Swiveling around in my stool, I said, "Excuse me, guys? Could you tell me what Fort Hall's known for?" It was the same icebreaker I always used.

One of them smiled and said, "Well, we call this place Fort Hallywood...where the stars come out at night." Both of them erupted in laughter. They loved a good joke, especially if they were the ones who told it.

Blaine and Lonnie were a couple of hardworking guys, who made a life for themselves chasing the American Dream. It just so happened that they were American Indians. Their families, who were part of the Shoshone-Bannock Tribe, had endured centuries of persecution, severe prejudice, profiling, stereotyping, and racism. They still do.

Suddenly, my life didn't seem so bad, and I knew why. It's all relative. We gauge the quality of our own lives by comparing them to others. When I'd ask cancer patients about having such a positive attitude, many of them would mention other patients who were in worse situations. Lonnie lost his father and grandfather to colon cancer. His grandfather wouldn't see a traditional white doctor because he believed in the "old peyote way." After everything he'd probably been through, I wouldn't blame him.

Lonnie and Blaine, Stars of Fort Hallywood.

I was glad to meet Lonnie and Blaine. Not because they were American Indians, not because they'd been affected by cancer, but because they were good, sincere people. They treated me with respect, regardless of what I looked like or who they thought I might've been. It felt good not to be judged, and I think Lonnie and Blaine understood that.

Southern Idaho near Rogerson.

CHAPTER 11

The
Silver State

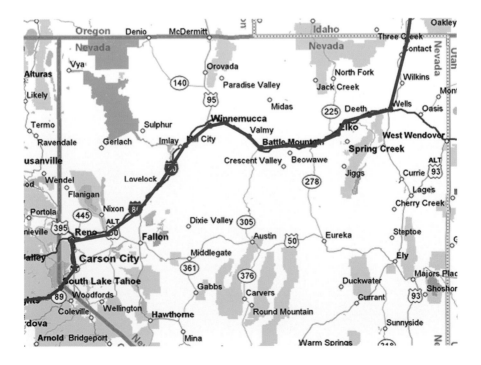

There were all kinds of things that I found on the side of the road, things people threw away, things people lost. Most of it was trash; cigarette butts, empty liquor bottles, fast food bags, clothing, and a wide variety of broken CDs and tapes. I also found some things worth keeping, like coins, jewelry, and other interesting knick-knacks. Of course, there was plenty of road kill. I even stumbled upon a whole cow carcass once. She must've gotten loose.

Northern Nevada was beautiful, but walking through it nearly drove me crazy. I'd look for things just to try and pass the time. The day I walked out of Winnemucca, I found four papa pennies, three quarters (one of them was bent completely in half), a silver dollar, a gold chain with the name 'Hector' engraved on it, a CB radio, and a small book entitled, *The Way to Happiness*.

The Way to Happiness...*in the desert...in Nevada.*

There were only two ways I could walk across Nevada: Interstate 80 or Highway 50. Neither would be easy, but the choice was simple. I wasn't about to walk on a highway dubbed 'The Loneliest Road.' Plus, I-80 was a straight shot to Reno. The Biggest Little City in the World was my light at the end of the tunnel, and getting there depended on a couple of Delta Sigs and two ladies in Lovelock.

The only problem with my plan was getting to Wells, where I-80 picked up. Wells was about 66 miles due south of Jackpot with nothing in between—no gas stations, restaurants, or any place to get food or water. It would be one of the few times I wasn't making any progress west. Giving myself three days to get the job done, I put Reno out of my mind and placed full priority on making it to Wells.

Getting right down to business, I knocked out several miles on the first morning. I wanted to walk 25 miles that day, but before I went any further, I'd have to deal with the maroon Chevy Tahoe that pulled off the road just ahead of me.

The moment when two guys got out, I knew Nick and Booch had kept their promises. They'd driven all the way from Pocatello, Idaho to help out a fraternity brother. I'm sure the idea of a road trip through Jackpot had something to do with it.

Our plan was simple. Nick and Booch would drive ahead and

stash supplies for the rest of my journey to Wells. On their way back, they stopped and walked with me for a mile or so.

A visit from my Pocatello posse meant a lot. I hadn't been able to count on everybody during the walk. Some people said they were going to bring water or meet me, but they never did. It may not have been important to them, but my life really depended on it. Nick and Booch weren't about to let me down.

My Pocatello Posse: Booch & Nick outside of Jackpot, Nevada.

That night, I set up camp only yards away from the highway. I was too tired to worry about someone stopping to see what I was doing. The temperature was dropping quickly, so I put on all of my clothes. At first, I thought it was unusually cold but remembered how deserts work—hot as hell during the day and 'freeze your ass off' cold at night.

This was beyond going into survival mode. Camping out every night like that in Nevada was going to kill me off. I pulled back my sleeping bag early the next morning so I could take a sip of water. It was frozen, just like the snot under my nose. It was going to be one of those days, but luckily, I had something to look forward to. I pulled out the directions Nick and Booch had given me.

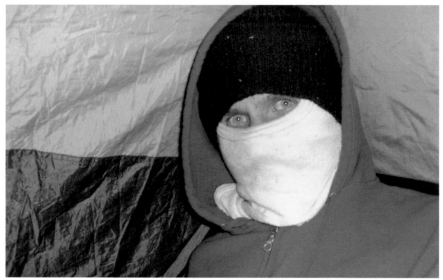

Hot days and cold nights in the Nevada desert.

On top of a hill, you'll see a 70-MPH speed limit sign on the right hand side.
There should be an old blue t-shirt tied to the bottom of the sign.
There's a hill to the right of the sign. Climb that hill.
You should find a cooler. Booty.

First Stash left by Nick and Booch.

After walking about 10 miles, I lost hope. I thought I must have passed it, but then I saw a road sign on top of the next hill. I found the treasure untouched, exactly where they said it would be. The cooler contained a gallon of water, fresh fruit, bread, energy bars, and an energy drink. I had a feast right there in the desert.

There was a lot of road construction that day. Car and trucks were backed up for miles. People would drive by me with shocked looks on their faces. They had a good point—who in the hell would be walking out there? In the middle of it all, I found the second stash. Just like they said, it was located behind a weather station on top of HD Summit. With all the road workers around, I thought someone would have already discovered the loot, but it was still there. Something sizeable had gotten to the fresh fruit, though. By the end of the day, I was about 12-15 miles out of Wells.

The next morning, I was soaking wet and sore. It had rained all night. Shortly after packing up my tent and hitting the road again, the weather took a turn for the worse. Chunks of ice were pounding every part of my body, and I had no place to hide.

In the spirit of Tyler, I screamed like a madman when I reached Wells. Getting there from Jackpot was the hardest thing I'd ever done. For that reason, I wanted to sleep in a real bed that night. I used my credit card to get a motel room. Because of the campaign, I was thousands of dollars in debt, but it was small price to pay for such a worthy cause. "C'est certain que vous avez besoin d'argent pour vivre mais pas pour aimer." *Certainly you need money to live but not to love.*

Wells was a good place to regroup. The first thing on my mind was taking a hot shower. When I got out, my cell phone was ringing. I smiled when I looked at the caller ID. It was someone I always loved to hear from. Vernie Davenport hadn't called in at least two weeks. The motherly concern in her voice warmed my heart.

"How are your feet," she said in her sweet southern voice. Telling her that they were fine was a lie, but I didn't want her to worry. Plus, my feet felt a lot better after the shower.

The rest of Nevada would be just as difficult, but at least I was heading towards Reno. Towns across the state were few and far between—more than I could walk in one day. Sometimes, the towns were several miles off of the interstate, which meant a lot of camping out in the middle nowhere.

Deeth was one of those places. There was nothing off of the exit, no homes, no gas stations, and I was out of water. Every now and again, a car or truck would get off of the exit, and I'd try to flag them down, hoping they would help me get some water. I'd lift my bottle and point at it, but the first six didn't even look at me. Finally, a woman driving a Cadillac looked over at me while she was driving by. When I lifted my bottle and smiled, she rolled her eyes and kept driving.

Camping in Deeth, Nevada.

My body didn't want to go any further without water, but I had no choice. I decided to try and flag down a Nevada Highway Patrolman. Finally, I could see one coming. I threw my arms in the air and nearly walked into the road. The officer turned his head slightly in my direction and blew right by me. He didn't even brake.

My mind was giving up. I had no prospects of finding water. Then I noticed some people working on an RV off of another empty highway exit. It was my best chance.

"Having some trouble?" I asked. I felt like an idiot asking such an obvious question, but it was the only way to break the ice. The man changing the tire didn't notice me, but the woman standing next to him did.

"Yeah, we got a flat," she said.

There was no point in beating around the bush, so I got straight to the point. "By chance, you wouldn't have any spare water, would you?"

The woman disappeared and came back with a couple of bottles.

"Pay it forward," she said handing them to me. I wanted to hug both of them.

Saved by some kind people fixing their RV near Halleck, Nevada.

"Is there anything I can do to help?"

"Nope, just pay it forward," she said.

It was a long and lonely road to Lovelock. Walking through the desert did something to my sense of distance. The land was so flat that I often thought towns were closer than they actually were. As one man in Battle Mountain put it, "You'll find all the towns 'round here look the same." Something that seemed only a couple of miles away was actually in the double digits.

Battle Mountain, Nevada in the distance.

Walking on the interstate was very lonely. There were all kinds of people out there, but they were driving by at 70-plus miles an hour. I waved every once in a while, sometimes they'd wave back, and sometimes they didn't. There was no one to talk to, and my cell phone didn't get service. I missed my family, I missed my friends, and most of all I missed Aimee.

When I walked into Lovelock, I stopped at a gas station to make a phone call. A man was standing by the pumps, filling up his truck.

"Was that you I saw walking out there?" He said.

"Yep," I smiled, happy to have a conversation with anyone.

"What're you up to?" He asked. It had been a while since I really told anyone about the walk.

Proudly I said, "I'm walking across the country to raise money for cancer research."

"It's not going to help," he said with a big grin.

"What?" I was caught off guard. He went on to tell me that billions of dollars were raised each year and that organizations like the American Cancer Society don't really want to find a cure.

"Believe me, I have friends in the business," he said replacing the gas nozzle on the pump. I thought about punching him out but decided he wasn't worth it.

"Thanks for the discouragement," I said sarcastically.

Whether what he said was true or not, I had already decided that this walk wasn't all about the money raised. It was about people like Wendy Bulter and Mary Jo Zyski of Lovelock. I would have never made it through the 40-mile desert without them. The 40-mile desert gets so hot, that settlers died trying to walk across it.

The 40-Mile Desert near Fernley, Nevada.

Even though it was October, it was very hot and dry. On my last night in the 40-mile desert, Wendy and Mary Jo brought me two spaghetti dinners and as much water as I could drink. It gave me the energy I needed to make Fernley.

From Fernley, Reno was within reach. I passed the Truckee River, which was the first natural water source I'd seen in weeks and for the first time in a long time, I believed in myself. If I could just get to Reno, I'd be home free.

My sister Brookelyn met me in Reno. She was the fourth and final sister to join me. Over a couple of days we walked to Carson City, which was 30 miles away.

Spending time with Brookelyn was exactly what I needed. You can really learn a lot about a sibling by walking through the desert

Reno, Nevada: The Biggest Little City in the World.

Brookelyn and Tilly Rogney in Reno, Nevada.

with them. When we got to Carson City, we visited the Carson-Tahoe Hospital. The next morning, she headed back to Las Vegas, but I found a note in my pack:

Eric-
I can't tell you how much fun this was for me. It feels really good to do this, helping other people and supporting what you do. I haven't belly laughed like that in months. There's someone looking over you. Or maybe you are an angel. Anyway I am so happy for you. This is the beginning of your career. You will be great. Now go eat a sandwich.

Love you so MUCH,
Brookelyn

P.s. You're almost there. See u in SF.

Finally, I was headed into California. It seemed like such a long time since I stepped off the beach in Nags Head. Soon enough, I'd see the Pacific. To finish off Nevada, I'd get to see another great body of water.

The road up to Spooner Summit wasn't very walker friendly. I had to tiptoe between traffic and a cliff. My feet were all chewed up when I reached the top, but the view was worth it. As I made my way down the mountain, I saw some water through some trees. Then I came to a larger opening and couldn't believe my eyes. Lake Tahoe was even more beautiful than I'd ever imagined.

Lake Tahoe.

CHAPTER 12

The Golden State

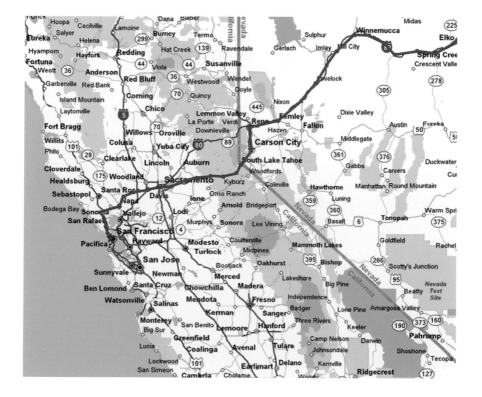

M edia coverage was very important. It meant I wasn't just some guy walking on the side of the road. More importantly, it helped raise money for cancer research and increased awareness, which literally saves lives. Many of the journalists that I spoke with had also been affected by cancer in some way. They were the real stories.

In my experience, there are two things that I know about photojournalists: they're not much for newsroom politics, and they're easy to talk to. Tony was a good guy, the kind you'd like to meet up with for the big game and a beer. He'd probably seen all kinds of things from behind the camera. After interviews, I'd always ask the journalists a question.

"Did you ever know anyone with cancer?" Tony nodded solemnly and started packing up his gear. Marcy, his news partner for the day, must have worked with him often.

"Tony lost his wife to breast cancer," she said.

I looked back at Tony and asked, "What was her name?"

Tony Toste and Marcy Valenzuela in Sacramento, California.

"Patti," he said. I'd seen the kind of look on his face a thousand times, the way we remember someone that we'd never see again. He was thinking about her face, her smile, the way she smelled, and all her nuances and idiosyncrasies that used to drive him crazy. Not all memories are good, and these were definitely painful for Tony.

∾

Ever since Nebraska, no matter how far west I got, people kept telling me, "It's all down hill from here."

I'd walked through the Dismal Swamp, the Appalachian Mountains, the Great Plains, the 40-Mile Desert, and the Rockies. There was only one more major geographic challenge between me and San Francisco—the Sierra Nevada Mountains.

After reaching Echo Summit, which was a mere 7,382 feet above sea level, it really was all down hill, and it was a gorgeous walk. During the day it was warm enough, but it started getting pretty cold at night. Fortunately I met some very friendly people who made sure that I didn't have to camp out.

The Sierra Nevada Mountains in California.

Sacramento was my last big city before the end. Reaching the capital of California meant I was less than two weeks away from San Francisco. I was almost there, but I never lost touch with what was most important—meeting people who were affected by cancer.

I was used to the standard procedures that go along with visiting cancer treatment centers. First you take a tour, then you meet the staff, and if you're lucky, you get to meet some patients. Don't get me wrong—the state of the art, high-tech, laser beam, x-ray, gamma splicer machines are very important in the fight against cancer, but more than anything, I always wanted to meet people.

So, when I was done taking the tour at UC-Davis Medical Center, I asked if I could meet any patients. The nurse went to check while I waited in the lobby.

"Hey, Tiger. Over here." An older man in one of the chairs was waving at me. He introduced himself as Grandpa Fassinger and kept right on talking.

"You look just like my grandson," he said, "I call him Tiger, too."

Without another word, he grabbed my right hand with both of his. Slowly, he looked up at me and said, "I'm gonna live through this. You know why?" I let the silence speak for itself.

"My sister says I have to," he replied sharply, "My older sister, she's 97 years old, and she says she's going to live to a hundred, and I've got to be there to see it." A big smile flashed across his face.

Grandpa Fassinger at UC-Davis Medical Center in Sacramento, California.

The World War II vet told me about his battle with Lymphoma, intertwined with tales of "The War." Grandpa Fassinger reminded me a lot of my own grandpa, someone with a wealth of knowledge and no one to share it with.

I never knew who I was going to meet or where I was going to meet them, so I shouldn't have been that surprised when a truck pulled up during my walk from Davis to Winters. There was a young woman with short, dark brown hair behind the wheel.

"Need a ride?" she asked with a smile.

"I can't," I said. "I've gotta walk."

"Why?" she asked.

"I'm about to finish a cross-country walk for cancer research." Suddenly, it really hit me that I was near the end. "I'm about to finish a cross-country walk for cancer research!

"Oh, wow—Right on, man!" She said enthusiastically. "Well, good luck!"

She pulled a U-turn and drove away. A few minutes later, I saw a person riding a bike toward me. It was the girl from the truck. She hopped off her bike and stuck out her hand.

"I'm Crystal," she said smiling, "I thought I should come out and walk with you for a while."

Sky Crazy Crystal near the Yolo County Airport in California.

Crystal walked with me for more than just a while. She walked with me for ten miles all the way into Winters. It was nice to have company. Crystal and I talked about everything, including her job. She packed parachutes for a drop zone at the Yolo County Airport.

When we got to Winters, Crystal introduced me to some of her friends from the drop zone. To say the least, they were adrenaline junkies. Some of those people had jumped out of a plane over a thousand times. Give them a little alcohol, and they come up with some crazy ideas. By the end of the night, they were trying to convince me to skydive the next morning. I told them it was out of the question. I was only eight days away from finishing. What if I got hurt and couldn't walk anymore?

I stayed at the drop zone that night. The next morning, we were all saying goodbye when I froze.

"I've gotta do this," I said softly.

"What?" Crystal asked.

"I've gotta do this. I've gotta jump," I said louder.

Crystal lit up. She grabbed my hand and ran with me to a classroom, where people were watching a video. I figured I'd have to do a little catch up, but after signing a few papers, Crystal was leading me somewhere else.

"Wait, what about the video?" I asked.

"Don't worry about it," she said, "We'll teach you how to jump later."

She wasn't lying. A little later, they gave me a crash course in jumping. Jim was my tandem partner. I think he was more excited than I was. Although it was my first jump ever, he insisted that I pull the chute.

"You'll be fine," he said pointing to the altimeter on my arm, "Just pull the chute at 55-hundred feet."

In a matter of 30 minutes, I had gone from saying goodbye to climbing into a plane. For some reason, I wasn't that nervous. It was all happening so fast.

When the prop came alive, I knew there was no turning back. Almost all of the people I met the night before were on the plane, which had climbed to 13,000 feet. I got my first rush when the bay door opened. The Pro's, who'd jump 20 times before the day was done, dove out the door gracefully. Then it was my turn.

Jim and I were sitting on the edge of the bay door. From that high, the green and brown sections of earth looked like an enormous

Just before climbing into the plane at Yolo County Airport near Winters, California.

quilt. He counted to three, and we plunged into thin air. I was screaming even though I couldn't hear myself. With his head positioned directly behind mine, I'm sure Jim didn't appreciate all the slobber coming from my mouth.

My heart dropped when we hit terminal velocity. The feeling of weightlessness was incredible. We were freefalling for about 60 seconds before I lifted my arm to look at the altimeter. It read 55-hundred feet, but for some reason, I didn't pull the chute. We hit 5,000 feet. Then we hit 45-hundred feet. Still nothing.

Finally, I pulled the chute at 4,000 feet, but it seemed like we were still falling pretty fast toward the earth. Jim, who had jumped hundreds of times, calmly said, "The chute's tangled—we need to shift our weight."

On the count of three, we shifted and the chute popped open. I was relieved to be floating toward the earth at a much safer 15-MPH. We were way off course, but I still got a couple minutes to enjoy the view. We had a rough landing in the dirt. Before taking off my gear, I called my mom.

"Hello?" She answered.

"Ma?"

"Eric!?" She was surprised. I hadn't called her in several days.

"Ma I just jumped out of a plane 13,000 feet above the earth, but I gotta go. Tell you 'bout it later."

"Wait, wait, wait," she said, but I hung up. I was too excited to talk on the phone.

What Sky Crazy Crystal said was true. Skydiving was the greatest rush I'd ever experienced in my life. The best part was, I did it for cancer research. When I got back to the jump zone, Jim handed me a packet. They had all pitched in to donate $70 to the American Cancer Society.

Camping for the first time in California near Circle Oaks.

For the rest of the day, I had an incredible adrenaline rush. I headed to Circle Oaks, which was just a small community of houses. I kept walking until sundown and put my tent next to a creek. It was the first time I had to camp in California. In some ways, I missed camping. I missed the privacy. I missed the serenity that nature provided. I missed reading to Michael.

Crossing California was fairly easy compared to Nevada or Wyoming. On the second to last day, I was walking to Mill Valley when I got a phone call from Cindy Collins. She and her family were riding around looking for me. Suddenly, a yellow cab pulled up as I was walking down a hill. I could see people waving through the windshield. It was Cindy, Kim, Stacy, Clayton, Kambry, and Collin.

I gave each one of them a hug as they piled out of the cab. It had stopped in the middle of the road, and traffic was backing up. Some cars were even honking their horns, but I didn't care. The Collins crew and I were having a moment. They walked with me for a few miles, and Kim even found a papa penny. There was no doubt in my mind that Dennis was with us the whole time.

Walking with Cindy Collins, Kim Nigg, Clayton Nigg, Stacy Orcutt, Kambry Orcutt, and Collin Orcutt.

A part of me didn't want to finish the walk. It had been challenging at times, but I was going to miss it—meeting new people every day, fighting for a cause that I believe in, and seeing beautiful parts of our country. I'm not sure what I expected to happen in San Francisco until I realized that the Golden Gate Bridge was simply an exclamation point at the end of a very long and complex sentence. I've never enjoyed the end of anything because to me, it's not the end. It's only the beginning of something new. The walk was just a snapshot in time.

My first look at the Golden Gate Bridge.

Matt Brennan, a survivor I'd met in Napa, was the first to meet me at the bridge. He brought his mom and his girlfriend Julie Flower. Then others started showing up. Four of my friends from college flew all the way from Washington D.C.: Juan Espinoza, Matt Hammond, Mike Banks, and Mike Sharkey. Maurice and Charlotte Morse flew in from Illinois, along with David and Theresa Wright and their family. Cindy Collins, Kim Nigg, Stacy Orcutt, Clayton Nigg, Kambry Orcutt, and Collin Orcutt were there as promised. Norm, Claudia, and Kevin Collins of Petaluma drove down. Wendy Butler and Mary Jo Zyski drove from Nevada. Several American

Cancer Society representatives showed up. And, of course, my sister Brookelyn kept her word. People from all over the country were there to walk across the bridge with me. Some I knew and many I didn't. Seeing all of those people confirmed the relationships that I'd made and further validated the walk.

"Bridge for a Cure" on the Golden Gate Bridge in San Francisco, California.

In a matter of minutes we made it across the bridge, but we didn't stop there. After a ceremony, a smaller group walked with me to Baker Beach. It was one of those special beaches where almost anything goes. Just as I was about to walk into the water, an older man lunged for a Frisbee right in front of me. He was completely naked. I made way for the nude exhibitionist, dropped my backpack, and finished my walk into the water, falling to my knees.

(*Photo Courtesy of Matt Brennan*)

By the time I reached San Francisco, I'd walked 3,591 miles over 206 days and raised more than $20,000 for the American Cancer Society. But more importantly, I met thousands of people who were affected by cancer. It was difficult watching them die, but it was worse watching them suffer. Through tragedy and triumph we shared many adventures.

As I was kneeling in the sand, staring out across the Pacific, one of my friends asked, "Think you'd do it again?"

"Anything's possible," I said sifting my hand through the sand. It was the end of one campaign and the beginning of another.

BRIDGE FOR A CURE

DENOUEMENT

Life is a journey of discovery, and I learned a lot during the walk. All of us expect certain things from certain people. We want our families to love us, our friends to support us, and strangers to respect us. That's what we want, but that's not always what we get. It all comes down to a contest of agendas, and I realized that there are five kinds that define relationships—yours, mine, shared, hidden, and default.

I thought my agenda was simple—to raise money for the American Cancer Society, but as I walked, my agenda changed. It wasn't about the money or an organization. It was about making a difference in the lives of people affected by cancer. Many people change their agendas after being diagnosed with cancer. They realize which relationships are important and gain a greater appreciation for life.

As a nation, there are certain agendas that we share, like fighting major diseases and promoting democracy. Sharing agendas can help build healthy and positive relationships. By working together, we can find a cure for cancer and achieve equality.

Not all agendas are known. Some people, organizations, and institutions carry hidden agendas, trying to get ahead by deceiving others. This can destroy relationships or even keep them from forming.

By default, we sometimes live life by other people's agendas, making decisions based on what they want or expect from us. We all let agendas control our relationships.

During the walk, I put myself in the hands of America, hoping that everything would turn out alright. It was a big risk. I didn't always know what people wanted, but I had to take that chance. My life depended on the kindness and compassion that I know lie within *all* Americans.

People took me into their homes and broke bread with me. They walked with me and shared their lives. They opened their hearts to me and because of that, I made thousands of friends and even fell in love.

The truth is, you never know who's going to walk into your life and change it forever.

THANK YOU

So many people contributed to the success of Walk About America 2005. Although I couldn't share everyone's story, all of these people are equally important and will forever remain in my heart. THANK YOU!

North Carolina: Carole Latham, Isabelle Blozis, Mark Latham, Al Crisp, Andy Brockmeyer, John of Mann's Harbor, Pete & Sunshine Gottfried, Art & Pauline Powell, Judy Mayo, Linda Dwyer, Charlie Dwyer, Buddy Oliver, Harvey Strickler, Samuel M. Harden, Aunt Tis-Is, Joseph & Elizabeth Cherry, Edith Parker (E-low), Brad Renegar, Michele Hewitt (Arkansas), Johnny & Rachel Pearce, Joe "Joe Cool" & Karen Coles, Michele Coles, Vernie Davenport, John & Jewell Glover, Chris Chin, Emily Snap, Joe & Joan Leotta.

Virginia: Dr. Keith R. Latham, Phyllis Latham, Angie Latham, Kleo Lane Texas, Caitlin Latham, Michael Latham, Corolyn Latham, Joe Street, Gary Moore, Domenick Casuccio, Allison Schooley, Pat Maehr, Austin Staples, Audrey Clayton, Angie Summerford, Massey Cancer Center, Carole Allen-Reynolds, Johnnie Boyd, Hannah Gallier, Drew Lichtenberger, The Wolf Hill Quilters, Abingdon High School, Judie Johnson, Barbara Fritzman, Celita Proffitt, Herb & Carla Proffitt, Amber Proffitt, E.O. "Slick" & Jean Greer, Luke Irby, Jenny, Brent & Elizabeth Miller, Roy Palmer Sr., Bobby Ray, Tina Ritzik, Anne Weiss, Debra Smiley, Harry & Darlene Craig, David & Helen Meinhard, Margaret Thomas, Martha Louis, Dan H. Edmonds (US Marine), Jim & Linda Fitzpatrick, James Fitzpatrick, Charlie Staples, Ben York, Patte Wood, Ginny Konchan, Kappa Sigma Fraternity (Washington and Lee University chapter), Chris

Pearce, Thomas G. Burrish, Beth Glenn, Bradley Vess, Chris & Jeanette Eberle, Clifton Forge Rescue Squad, Nancy McCutchen, Christy Jeffries, Laura Booze, Lula Gilbert, Jim Sherlock, Dawn Wilson, Sharon Montgomery, Donnie Wheatley, Jeff Baker, Terry Michael Banks Jr., Michael Sharkey, Evan Yeager, Delta Sigma Phi Fraternity (Kappa Delta Chapter, Virginia Tech), Robyn Chandler, Nick Malcolm, Marty & Lowanna Link, Randy & Darlene Newlon.

West Virginia: Geraldine Mosley, Debra Simmons, Francis & Margie Hammond, Matt Hammond, Don Hammond, Bob & Lorrie Hammond, Lioness Club of Lewisburg, Mary Jane Gilkerson, Juan Espinoza, Becky Tipton, Joyce LaRue, Mayor Charlie Mundy, Rupert Fire Chief Dalton Elmore, Pauleetia Fisher, Dr. Vivian Crane, Debbie Goddard, Carol Parker, Margaret Darby, Cynthia Martin, John Cohenour, Tony Bryant, Calvin Braggs, Wanda Ross, C.G. Flint, Allison Flint, Bob & Jean Wells, Don & Judy Miller, Shannon Harrell, Lloyd Harrell, Frank George, Carla Lucas, Karen Newman, Hedy Chapman, Nathan King, Don & Wilma Dobbins, Kevin Tephabock, Mike McKee, Abbigail Grace Hodge, Buddy & Andrea Hodge, Dalton Hodge, Mam-Ma Lois A. King, Charleston Area Medical Center Women and Children's Hospital, Christi Bissett, Erin Craffey, Michele Smith, Andrew & Hallie Dunlap, Cora Dunlap, Bobby Taylor, Betsy Allen, Calvert McNeely, Randy Tidd, Robin Chaney, Linda Carter, Randall Price, Barbara Price, Anthony Johnson, Eileen O'Leary, Jay Stephenson, Ron LeMaster, Cliff Hankins, West Huntington Fire Station, Scot Masters, Scott Jeffries, Tim Salyers, Rick Miller, Justin Sanders, Tim Provoznik, Toby Mitchell.

Kentucky: Aimee Elizabeth Reed, Jewell Gilette, Barbara Payne, Sylvia Foreman, Jonell Curreli, Debbie Broughton, Craig Sloan, Anita Hale, Gwen Barker, Mark Hamilton, Willie Patton, Brent Porter, Fran Henderson, Carla Emerson, Randy Sholars, Mike Williamson, Denver Brown, Gayle Sparks, Ethel Callahan, Mitch Hamm, Teresa Dehart, Tania Sexton, Carol Carter, Shy (my "Canine for Cancer Research), Fran Henderson, Joe Vanderpool, Lauren Routt, Lindsay Routt, Erin Willis, Janie Corbin, Tommy Willoughby, Jim Hornback, Brent Porter, Kristie Jenkins, Travis

Brown, Montgomery County Senior Citizens Center, Betty Elliot, Lorena Shoemaker, Kathy Hayes, Clyde & Janet Jones, Sam, Linda Elam, Todd Denham, Betty Ratliff Smith, Laverne Yates, Judy Hatch, Ric Larson, Richie Holmes, Kyle Sloan, Craig Sloan, Jacob Cannon, Thomas Cannon, Barbara Minix, Reverend David & Kim Calhoun, Judy Chase, Caren Callahan, Steven & Brenda Reffett, Grace Williams, John Williams Jr., Brent Wooten, Jennie Bentley, Brian Tyler, Bo & Joy Lanter, Velva Templeton, Joe Charles, Gene Oakley, Tears, Randy & Cindy Clark, Dexter Chappel, John & Kathy Chilton, Karen Swayer-Messier, Debbie Howes Fleming, Molly Williamson, Amy Wallot, Georgann Conway, Ben Koch, Leroy & Karen Koch, Hannah Koch, Carol Wade, Marilyn Lesher, Shawn Brown, Lafond Wright, Diane Jessee and her three children, Mac, Bill, and Leah; Britton Reid, Fred Brown, Robert Duggins, Megan Kaleher, Rosalind Brennam, Bernard & Baron (Kosair), Joy Chambers, Sandy & Kevin (Kosair), Andrew (Kosair), Kosair Children's Hospital, Alan Reed.

Indiana: Charlotte & Maurice Morse, David & Theresa Wright, Jo Sparks, Clive Chan, Mark & Colleen Wright, Wilma Stepp, Edith G. (Clarksville), Dave & Darlene Wolkow, Ruby Booth, Jason & Jami Poore, Craig Padgett, Andy Jones, Rich McGinnis, Jimmy McConahay, Shari Hardy, Mike Amrhein, Glenn Pence, Kathy Baker, Alex Spicer, Roscoe Barnett, Jennie Witten, William Toppe and his dog Lucy, Robert Young, Ron Crumbo, Donna Minnick, Pru Cooley, Brian Blair, Judy Belle, Kayla Belle, Erin at Franklin College, Sue Padgett, Sherrie Conner, Officer Steve Stalets, Kristie Bayliss, Dawn Ohns, Marcus Keys, Joni Emmert, Delta Sigma Phi Fraternity, Scott Riley, Nathan Wight, Riley Children's Hospital, Indiana University Hospital, John Mills, Willard Douglas Gibbons, Mildred Smith, John & Adrienne Jackson, Bob & Judy Stadfeld, Sue Whiting, Jessie Rae and her boyfriend Jared, Caleb Arthur, John Helling, Larry Hathaway, Crawfordsville Public Library Barbara Nolan, Nadine Sample, Marilyn Sowers, Jenny Hayman, Virginia Hardesty, Kay Ward, Gary Cox.

Illinois: Dennis & Cindy Collins, Roy & Kim Nigg, Clayton Nigg, Donnie & Stacy Orcutt, Kambry Orcutt, Collin Orcutt, Sheila

Blacketer, James & Amie Morse, Le Roy & Bertie Moore, Carle Hospital and Cancer Center (Urbana), Cindy Stiger, Sonya Green, Lindsay Stiger, Andrew Pyle, Melissa Phillips, Amanda Gooden, Mary Van Cleave, Kate Garbacz, Caroline Woodis, Sandy Galbreath, Cat Tice, Erik Potter, Dorothy Canard, Jessie DeHaan, Morgan DeHaan, John Amdor, Joe Amdor, Rick Dean, Don & Wanda Dean, Steve Ward, Warren Herberger, Steve Moran, Joellen Adams, Chris LaFever, Laura Adam, Carmen Prochnow, Pete & Cindy Avery, Maureen Barnosky-O'Conner, David Lyons, Tim Meredith, Jessica Gieson, Autumn Thomson, Frances Price, Jeri Andrew, Jim Bortell, Rose Ornduff, Jeremy Dabbs, Jordan Beres, Brenda Skelton, Lori Martin, Terese Engling, Daniel Engling, Max Engling, Dave Irvin, Sharie Mabry, Dave Irvin, Theresa Shields, Harold Breitenbach, Paul Grant, Jack Felts, Dan Kelly, Bob Eid, Sam Eid, Duane Greer, Ali Majd, Maurice Brown, Kevin Ludolph, Mike Baker, Brimfield Public Library, Sarah Fisher, Kevin Wertz, Anthony & Dawn Mannino, Mike Burns, Josh Kramer, Dan Leonard, Dell Leonard, Dr. Gary Zwicky, Gary & Deb Gehring, Scott Gehring, Kaylan Gehring Art Pitsonbarger, Ann Boyer, Barbara Conner, Cordell & Jenny Johnson, Irene Brown, Phyllis Boerger, Miriam Manyara, Kris Russell, Darlyce Russell, Jean Jacobs, Kent Kriegshauser, Chris Etheridge, Cody Johnson, Dan & Heather Johnson, Tim Holt, Tom Dennis, Tom Doubleday, Dirty Timmy's, Bruce Curry (Bruce-O-Lantern), Wilma Carroll, Stanley Weber, Sandy Snyder, Louise Nelson, Kaitlyn Jane Boney, Gerry & Valerie Garrison, Sarah Betsworth, Diana Betsworth, James & Lisa Betsworth, Becki Maxson, Jack & Marilyn Gross, Trinity Cancer Center, Mary Lundeen, Bonnie Parchart, Ron & Janet Marshall, Christina Nall, Dale Whitcanack, Pat Whitcanack, Marguerite Miller, Cheryl Trent, Jane Smith, Dr. Michael Porubcin, Dr. Lawrence W. Allen, Deb Petersen, Mary Mangels, Jerry & Kathy Frank, Edith Quayle, Patricia Croegaert, Nina Williams, Grant McCombs.

Iowa: Tyler Weig, John Freeman, Marty Ellison, Carole Coy Kendall, Brett Hamilton, Carl Shoot, Becca Jeffers, Ben Trott, Stephanie Trott, Josh Trott, Ann Pelley, Wendy, Will and Jennifer at Slaby's Bar and Grill (Plain View), Doc and Kate (Plain View), Dean

& Cindy Lund, Marlin & Pat Hillyer, Jodi Byrd, Richard Byrd, Spencer Byrd, Ashley Byrd, Nathan Countryman, Lois Conway, Maggie Challis, Gwen Drahos, Valerie Wyldes, Jacque Stovall, Mark & Kathy Banowetz, St. Luke's Hospital (Cedar Rapids), Pam McDaniel, Darrel & Deanna Sanden, Isabelle Thomas, Mark Harvey, Steve Gravelle, Theresa Driskell, Nikki Morgan, Mary Conner, Patty Shaffer, Sue Hadenfeldt, Nancy Camp, Glen & Valerie Wallace, Bill Hurley, Scott Fowler, Kari Niner, Tyanna Stephenson, Art Dunkel, Cheryl Propst, Bob Kendall, Casey Jesina, Monica Fogle, Owen Kapayou, Erin Ackerman, Samson Keahna, David Brown, Nathan Taylor, Jill Taylor, Shirley Taylor, Stephanie Snow, Kary Berg, Ben Harapat, Terry & Linda Fristoe, Curt & Linda Smith, Dick & Janet Vaudt, Phil Gould, Elly Mack, Amber Illum, Claire Hanken, Casey Henderson, Ben Anderson, Dave Sowers, House of Compassion (Marshalltown), Mark Ferren, Linda Smith, Pat McIntosh, Dennis Vaughn, Chris Vaughn, Joanie Jamison, Doug Vaughn, Darin Tissue, Juel Haaland, Todd & Jane Holcomb, Ted Tedesco, Roman Lynch, Mark & Pauline Johnson, Dean & Marilyn Hill, Mike & Linda Halbach, Kathy Pierce, Leon & Kay Wittrock, Ken Norem, Elaine Chiles, Tammy Tiffany, Cynthia Cowden, Tori Charge, Matt Rozell, Dr. Laura Myers, CoAnne Hartman, John & Dorothy Zimmerman, Peter Youngren, Randy Riesburg, Barry Moeller, Chuck Signs, Jerry Reiman, Carol Smith, Todd Donner, Katie Farrell, Don Dauphanis (MA), Michael Baxa, Jeff Naeve, Sandy Haynes, Donna Erlbacher, Dewey Hupke, Norman Carlson, Mary Ann Savery, Peggy Carlson, Tena Henkel, Ted Mallory, Bekah Shupe, Don Haahr, Helen (Grandma Whimpy), Alma Green, Andrew Pearson, Johnny Shattuck, Lauri Chase, Leslie Hansen, St. Luke's Hospital (Sioux City), Bomgaar's Cancer Center (Sioux City), Rod Ketelson, Roger Bomgaars, Bomgaars Stores, Larry & Annie Martinson, June E. Nylon Cancer Center (Sioux City), Pat Hubbard, Michelle Erickson, Carol Walton, Nancy Barker, Jennifer Brown, Catherine Saulsburg, Cindy McClary, Karen Johnson, Linda Lanphier, Karen Van De Steeg, Susan Chapman, Irene Markey, Cole Barker, Patricia Neal, Leann Williams, John Arnt, Donna Thogersen, Jessie Stanislav, Joan Samson, Ruth Sick, Ron "Smiley" Anderson, Lee Kirkpatrick, Ellen Golden, Alex Gleason, Lyle & Verla Collison, Norma Courtney, Bill Wonder, Laura McDole, Perry

Thrift, Sergeant Patrick Horn, Lois Johnson, Marcia Brandt.

Nebraska: Gary Huffman, Susan Smith, Jan Huffman, "Toolie", Helen Koopman (WI), Theresa Kleinowski (WI), Betty Olson (WI), Jane Nazaretian (WI), Frank Holliday, Larry McCulloch, Vinny Arnold, Darren Snow, Sam & Lori Titus, Leon Bowlind, Bill Bowlind, Lois Robinson, Linda Bisunz, Jake Rasperson, Laura Stloken, Tammy Saltzman, Lorraine Hansen, Brooke Kobs, John & Ann Kobs, Rev. Shirley Schmidt, Eleanor Buchhardt, Sandy Miller, Maria of Los Compadres, Randy and Linda Papendick, Marlene Hartman, Delores, Andel, Majorie Bailey, Mildred Salak, Allison Aldrich, Gerry Sagehorn, Jerome & Judy Jakub, The Steinics (Havens), Jasmine, Rich & Joy Savage, St. Francis Medical Center (Grand Island), Chief Jack Bowen, Eliodoro "Lefty Salinas, Florentino Salinas, Dan & Susan Wolfe, Brenda Bender, Good Samaritan Hospital Cancer Center (Kearney), Sarah Schaef, Albin "Shub" & Diana Shubert, Laurie Cicotello, Pam Ackerman, The Soroptomists (Lexington), Carl Kyle, Jim Ostergard, John & Elaine Schlake, Trent & Misty Schlake, Eddie "The Walker," Kim & Brett (Maxwell), Jess Feltz, Sandy Edwards, Chris Jurgens, Chuck & Barbara Bauee, Peter Jennings, Herb & Sandy Meissner, Kim Schneider, Marge Perlinger, Leanna Kramer, Pastor Curtis & Janean Tschetter, Steve Olofson, Josh Mackey, Matt Schick (KS), Bill Rudel, Hank Smith, Julia Beisner, Joe & Cindy Van Newkirk, Brad & Lana Batt, Leroy & Peg Stevens, Mason Stevens, Cherry Stevens, Ryan & Rachel Patterson, Melody Duran, Russ & Sharon Orosz, Cancer Center at Scottsbluff Regional Medical Center, Dr. Mark Hartman, Ione Beavers, Ross Johnson, Carissa McNabb, Jeannine Grubb, Orvin & Dorothy Hicks, Julia Meissner, Vicki Allen, Blanca Bair, Pam Crane, Victoria Pavlista, Jerry & Veronica McDaniel, Larry Hubbard, Carol Diffendaffer, JoAnn Cervantes, Cindy Keller, Debra Schneider, Donny Sylvester, Jayme Hawk, Jennifer Childress, Connie & Duane Svobeda, Bob & Sue Van Newkirk.

Wyoming: Tracy Davis, Shelly Duncan, Valerie Grant, Julene Asmus, Eldon & Jodi Garver, Cliff & Vera Thompson, Alex Meyer, Brenna Clossen, Kat Clossen, Floyd Moore, Judi Skeen, Harley Hughes (Harley's Angels), Bobbi Larsen, Annie (Glenrock), Vicki

Haley, Rocky Mountain Oncology (Casper), Marty Brammer, Terri Sharp, Becky Childress, Pamela Carrell, Abbie Libel, Angie Van Houten, Dr. Robert Tobin, Gail Enyert, Pam Brewer, Kim Berdahl, Nikki (Casper), Bill Leach, Vern and the Help for Health Bus, Marva (Casper), Bob the Volunteer, Blanche Bednarz, Raymond Shain, Monte Johnson, Miles Johnson, Ila Johnson, Betty Krause, Nancy Fluegel, Rita Miller, Le Ron Coleman, Tom & Pat Kaiser, Toni Benthusen, Mike Murphy, Mike Vigil, Stanley Simmons, Guy McCurdy, Ken Ballard, Roy Smith, Charles B. Smith, Bob & Carla Steelman, Lee & Carlene Weiss, Harry & Judy Hurt, Rascal Flatts, Steve Boehler, Chris Robertson (TX), Ariel Crichton, Ann Crichton, Marcia Howard, Chris & Dana Harr, Diana Rose, Larry Barrett (OR), Lloyd Mollingboll, Wayne Nichols, Patrick & Karen O'Kane (MN), Deputy Brady Patrick, Tigger, Reverend Charles Taylor, Rick & Echo Klaproth, Krizinne Cross, Heidi Meyer, Uma & Flossy, Martin Kennedy, Ned & Amanda Pinkerton, St. John's Hospital Oncology Center (Jackson Hole), Carole Poole, Judy Bayse, Paige Janssen, Floyd & Shirley Harvey (TN), Clarene Law, Emiley Knobloch, Dr. John Ward (UT), Mark Mickelson.

Idaho: Kara Donnelly, Keith "Skeeter" Cattabriga, Luke, Grove & Timanee Becker, Daryl & Wendy Duttenhoeffer, Mark Stiteler, Jon Wetzel, Catherine Traverso, Cancer Center at Eastern Idaho Regional Medical Center, Dr. Calvin McAllister, Jim & Ellen Guymon, Cindy Guymon, Jim Kluvers, Ryan Thatcher, Rosemary Yerke, Lonnie Marshall, Blaine Edmo, Janice Pebeashy, Timothy Kinney, Nick Hutt, "Booch" Vannavong, Odell & Roselind Byington, Cancer Center at Portneuf Medical Center, David Theel, Bill Schaefer, Dan Boyd, Leslie (Burley), Sven Lundberg (OR), Dewayne & Georgie Wagemen, Mike & Peggy Connelly, Fred & Shawneen Gannaway.

Nevada: Brookelyn Latham, John Bristow, Scott Taylor, Dale & Sam Feltman, Shawn Feltman, Debi & Jimmy Geradt, Ron & Joanie Owens, Shane Hansen, Thomas Arp, Mike Grigg, Alan & Patty Rowe, Art & Rhonda Minchew, Becky Glennon, Kerry Aguirre, Mike Timm, Paul Gracey, Ellen Aker, Forrest Newton, David Lewis, Paul Copeland, Gwen Carter, Wendy Butler, Mary Jo Zyski, Mac

Potter, Theresa & David Wilson, Bill Frankmore, Kausik Bhakta, Zach Patterson, Maja Rogney, Tillie Rogney, Kyle Davis, Washoe Medical Center (Reno), Val & Pearl Young, Rick & Cathy Martin, Carson-Tahoe Regional Medical Center, Lindsey Jackson, Kory & Denise Davis, Carson-Tahoe Cancer Resource Center, Patrick Williams, Karen Woodmansee, Chien Chung Cheng, Wen Shi Cheng, Toni Pardee, Dottie Kellher, Patricia Buckler, Michelle Rowan, Kristen Smith.

California: Brian Bilbrey, Anne Koelling, Jeff Munson, Susan Wood, Al from New Guinea, Linda Harper, Chris Sneed, Alan Gregory, Tim DeVoe, Arlene Kolberg, Peter Swanson, Milton & Millie Thorman (M&M), Arnt & Donna Krogstad, Tony Toste, Marcy Valenzuela, Gayle Matthews, Sutter Cancer Center (Sacramento), Phyllis Ragsdale, Marcella (Sacramento), John & Donna Conner, Theresa Eve, UC-Davis Cancer Center (Sacramento), Grandpa Fassinger, Reid & Eileen Selover, Claudia Morain, Robert Valenzuela, Kevin Swartz, UC-Davis Chapter of Delta Sigma Phi, Sky Crazy Crystal, Sky Dance Sky Diving (Davis), Wayne Beebe, Lars Anderson, Bob & JoAnn Myers, Matt Brennan, Julie Flower, Torrey Schoen, Queen of the Valley Hospital Cancer Center (Napa), Pat Stanley, Butter Crème Bakery, James O'Reilly, Cathey Colelli, Sandra Dudley, Tina Harrison, Norm & Claudia Collins, Jim & Nancy (Petaluma), Jim & Mary Wyrick, Kevin Collins, Monica Holbrook, Kellie Holbrook, Wally & Joan Rentsch, Linda Garoutte, Chris Wopperer, Meagan Nolan, Rita Burns, Bob Harper, Michael Bishop, Colin Osiecki.

Numbers

Miles walked: 3591

Days walked: 206

Money raised for the American Cancer Society: $21,923.59

Cans redeemed for cancer research donations in Iowa: 187 at 5 cents a piece ($3.30)

Number of Days Papa Pennies found: 87

Number of Days Nanny Nickels found: 28

Most miles walked in one day:

34 (from near Guernsey, WY to Glendo, WY)

32 (from Buckingham Courthouse, VA to Amherst, VA)

Most miles walked in two days:

64 (from Guernsey, WY to Glendo, WY and from Glendo, WY to Douglas, WY)

54 (from Jefferson, IA to Carroll, IA and from Carroll, IA to Denison, IA)

Least miles in a walking day:

8 miles (Onawa, IA to Decatur, NE)

10 miles (Hollister, ID to Rogerson, ID)

Mile Markers:

Reached 500 miles near Ansted, WV

Reached 1000 miles near Lizton, IN

Reached 1500 miles near Ogden, IA

Reached 2000 miles near Roscoe, NE

Reached 2500 miles near Dubois, WY

Reached 3000 miles near Elko, NV

Reached 3500 miles near Winters, CA

Miscellaneous:

Ticks found on body: 22

Times pulled over by police officers: 34

Times pulled over by police officers and asked for ID: 15

Pairs of Montrail boots used: 2 (the first pair last 1,962 miles into North Platte, NE)

Chased by dogs: 11

Flipped off: 5

Swerved at by a vehicle: 2

Fireworks thrown at me by a person in a passing vehicle: 1

Taco thrown at me: 1

Full Pepsi thrown at me: 1

Rides offered for progress: 271

Cried: 8

Offered a gun to take with me: 1

Offered Marijuana: 2

Vehicle accidents witnessed: 3 (Lewisburg, WV; Seymour, IN; Scranton, IA)

Asked to buy beer for minors: 1 (Charleston, WV)

Times taken a # 2 in the wilderness: 19

Toenails lost: 7

Rubber bracelets given to me: 24

Pins given to me: 17

Given a pedicure: 1

Strange Places to Sleep:

Slept in SUV: 1 (Lewiston, NC)

Slept on porch: 1 (Montgomery, WV)

Slept in fire stations: 2 (Huntington, WV and Ashland, KY)

Slept in library: 1 (Brimfield, IL)

Slept in barn: 1 (Henry, NE)

Slept in RV: 2 (Havens, NE and Idaho Falls, ID)

Highest Altitude Reached:

9,658 feet above sea level
(Togwatee Pass, WY on September 5, 2005)

8,431 feet above sea level
(Teton Pass, WY on September 10, 2005)

7,382 feet above sea level
(Echo Summit, CA October 20, 2005)

7,146 feet above sea level
(Spooner Summit, NV on October 18, 2005)

6, 917 feet above sea level
(Dubois, WY on September 4, 2005)

5, 998 feet above sea level
(Hiland, WY on August 28, 2005)

3,175 feet above sea level
(Sewell Mountain, WV on May 12, 2005)

2,542 feet above sea level
(near Clintonville, WV on May 11, 2005)

Lowest Altitude Reached:

40 feet below sea level
(Luck Stone Quarry in Manakin, VA on April 29, 2005)

Weight Loss:

Weight in September 2004
(when I created Walk About America): 205 lbs.

Weight on April 14, 2005
(when I started walking from Nags Head, NC): 188 lbs.

Weight in Lewisburg, WV: 175 lbs.

Weight in Montgomery, WV: 170 lbs.

Weight in Lexington, KY: 172 lbs.

Weight in Scottsburg, IN: 165 lbs.

Weight in Urbana, IL: 169 lbs.

Weight in Peoria, IL: 168 lbs.

Weight in Tipton, IA: 172 lbs.

Weight in Ute, IA: 168 lbs.

Weight in Kearney, NE: 165 lbs.

Weight in Shoshoni, Wy: 163 lbs.

Weight in Elko, NV: 165 lbs.

Weight in Sacramento, CA: 168 lbs.

Weight in San Francisco, CA: 170 lbs.

HOW TO ORDER

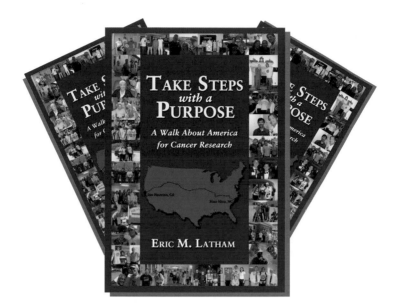

To order copies of *Take Steps with a Purpose,* visit www.takesteps-withapurpose.com to make a secure credit card payment or send a check or money order for $34.95 each, along with your mailing information, to:

Walk About America
15120 Industrial Park Rd.
Bristol, VA 24202

Your support and contributions are what allow Eric Latham and **Walk About America** to continue enhancing community awareness and involvement across the United States.

—